Indispensable
by
Monday

Indispensable
by
Monday

LEARN THE PROFIT-PRODUCING BEHAVIORS THAT WILL HELP YOUR COMPANY . . . AND YOURSELF

LARRY MYLER

WILEY

John Wiley & Sons, Inc.

Published by John Wiley & Sons, Inc., Hoboken, New Jersey.
Published simultaneously in Canada.

For general information on our other products and services or for technical support, please contact our Customer Care Department within the United States at (800) 762-2974, outside the United States at (317) 572-3993 or fax (317) 572-4002.

Wiley also publishes its books in a variety of electronic formats. Some content that appears in print may not be available in electronic books. For more information about Wiley products, visit our web site at www.wiley.com..

Library of Congress Cataloging-in-Publication Data:

Myler, Larry, 1959-
    Indispensable by Monday: learn the profit-producing behaviors that will help your company—and yourself/Larry Myler.
        p. cm.
    ISBN 978-0-470-55477-7 (cloth)
    1. Organizational effectiveness.   2. Cost effectiveness.   3. Value added.
4. Employee motivation.   I. Title.
    HD58.9.M95 2010
    650.1—dc22

                                                                    2009038780

Printed in the United States of America

10 9 8 7 6 5 4 3 2 1

To Jill, Rachelle, Trey, Conner, Marissa, and Lauren.
Thank you for your unfailing support and confidence.

Contents

Part 3 Making It All Work . . . Starting Monday Morning   133

Foreword

My company, VitalSmarts, has grown both revenues and profits at an average of 25 percent per year for the past decade, and I am convinced that if you seriously infuse the ideas in this book into the DNA of your organization, so will yours.

I attribute our success to two things:

1. First, we have developed potent solutions to persistent client problems.
2. Second, we have worked with skilled employees who think and act like owners and who know how much attention is required to keep the bottom line healthy.

Frankly, I've discovered that the former is far more easily attained than the latter. If you're an owner, leader, manager, or supervisor in an organization who has already figured out the first point, this book will help you achieve the second. If you're an employee who is looking to increase your value and become a contributor your company can't live without, you have come to the right book. Conversely, you may be unemployed and looking for a tangible advantage over many other job candidates. Well, here it is.

The assertion that the first challenge of entrepreneurship is finding a market you can serve better than anyone else—and the second is creating an employee team that is wildly passionate and supremely capable of growing and improving the company—may sound simple. But strangely, while all leaders know they've got to get number one right, most have no idea how vital number two is. I once worked in a company that got job one right and totally ignored job two. The company's sales expanded nicely; in fact, the product was so good that we grew from zero to $100 million in about 10 years. The problem, however, was that we never made a profit.

My partners and I learned a powerful lesson by watching this company's experience. And when the time came to set out to start our own, we decided to work hard on Larry Myler's prescription. We committed to being uncompromising about placing the right people in the right jobs and spending any effort required to equip them with all that they needed to act like owners at all times. The results have been more than worth the investment.

So, ask yourself the following questions:

- How much would it be worth to you as a business leader to have a graphic designer so wildly committed to your success that he sells your products to his weekend ski students? Our graphic designer, Kevin, closed more than one deal for us in exactly this way.

- How much would you invest to get an events coordinator who is so animated about reducing costs that she finds a way to negotiate tens of thousands of dollars in savings from your hotel suppliers? I'm convinced Janet falls asleep at night dreaming up new ways to do more with our precious resources.

- How many more sales would your company have to make to equal the profit contribution of your shipping department— doubling its capacity without adding a dime to costs? Nate did precisely that for our company last year.

I am convinced that after your company finds its market niche, the most important work you can do is to ensure that every single employee in your company can do what Larry Myler describes in these priceless pages. And if you're not a leader—but "just" an employee—*pay attention to this story.*

In her short career of five years in our company, Mary has doubled her income. She didn't do so by getting annual cost-of-living adjustments, playing politics, or staying busy doing non-value-added, made-up work. She didn't win the lottery, and she certainly didn't do it by negotiating harder for promotions. Instead, she relentlessly asked and answered the simple question at the heart of this important book: *How can I add more value?* Because of that, Mary is literally indispensable.

At the end of every year, my partners and I go over a list of names of those we are terrified could be poached by shrewd competitors. We talk long and hard about what we're doing to ensure that these vital employees are being fairly compensated and are given the autonomy they need to thrive in our company. Mary is at the top of that list.

Every few months, Mary will make an appointment with me to learn more about the future direction of the company. Then, she'll reassess her priorities to ensure that her work is aimed at significantly accelerating our progress in that direction. If it's reducing costs, Mary becomes an alchemist for clever ideas. If the challenge is to expand our reach, she tirelessly uncovers new opportunities we can exploit. She is truly Indispensable with a capital "I."

In my view, the title of this book is no false promise. It is, in fact, the natural consequence of applying the sound, proven, and timeless behaviors that Larry Myler teaches so masterfully. I had the benefit of being tutored in these concepts personally by Larry himself over a 10-year period, and I've long suspected that unless you could have him at your elbow, there was no way to gain the wisdom he had to offer. You can imagine how thrilled I was to see how successfully he distilled decades of entrepreneurial brilliance into this compact and fascinating volume. Diligent readers can now compress my 10-year mentorship into a much more efficient learning curve.

So, if you've already done job one, I urge you to absorb and apply these concepts with all the energy they deserve. I trust that the payoff in your career and your business will match—or even exceed—my own.

And as much as I'm confident of the personal benefit you'll gain, my deeper hope is that this book becomes required reading for every leader and employee on the planet. If successful businesses are the engine of economic, social, and political progress in the world, then Larry Myler's prescription provides the power to drive that which we care most about.

To your success!

Joseph Grenny
Provo, Utah

Preface

Why I Wrote This Book

The vast majority of advice you can find on topics like getting a job, keeping your job, or being promoted is—for lack of a better term—fluff. By and large, it's mostly about political, non-value-added tactics that don't bring more dollars to the company's bottom line. You will come across countless lists of things to do, including wearing nice shoes and having a bright smile. You'll be told to get to work in the morning before the boss arrives and leave after he or she does. You may even be persuaded to eat lunch at your desk and just look busy all the time—by doing *anything*. If you buy into this pervasive pop mentality, you may feel it necessary to volunteer for everything and generally make yourself more "visible." But what you *really* need to do is help the company earn more money than it spends and spend less than it earns—period.

Look, if you're already coming to work on time and with clothes on and are a fairly decent colleague who does pretty well at your job description, then you can best help yourself by adding real, hard-dollar value to your company—*now*.

By taking advantage of what you're about to find within the pages of this book, you will absolutely be more valuable to your employer (or prospective employer). It doesn't matter what the economy is like. Creating profit for your company is always your best approach, in good times or bad. The only difference is that in bad times, you will be more likely to get or keep a job, and in good times, your chances of being promoted or receiving pay raises and bonuses will increase. Said another way, this book was not written to work in a specific economy but rather in *every* economy.

Believe it or not, these concepts will likely be even more valuable in good times than in bad. That is because when the economy is so good that all a company has to do to make money is be open for business, leaders and employees alike tend to get lax and forget about running a tight ship. And that is the time when your personal profit contributions can drive your organization's bottom line forward even more impressively.

So, get dressed, smile, and make sure you leave for work on time. But if visibility is your goal, arm yourself with what really matters: the skills, knowledge, ability, and tools you need to become *Indispensable by Monday!*

Cheers,

Larry Myler
www.moreorlessinc.com

Acknowledgments

If you've never locked yourself in a room with four MBAs and one attorney for two hours a week over a three month period, you should. It's not as bad as it sounds . . . quite nice, actually. Many thanks to Darryl Wagner, Rob Storey, Tod Bybee, David Rasmussen, and Heather McDougald for offering invaluable help in vetting and refining the concepts that made it into print, and mercifully killing the ones that didn't.

To fellow workers who brilliantly bring financial benefits to clients, and who have made contributions to this effort, I offer my respect, thanks and admiration: Cheryl Snapp Conner, Chris Jordan, Josh Rowley, Cory Maloy, Tom Pittman, Jim Murphy, Brent Hirschi, Steve Glover, Russ Warner, Kevin Simister, and Joe Thomas.

First-round edits would not have been nearly as fun without Cami Buhman. Proofreading and excellent improvements were graciously offered by Mike Carter, Steve Glover, Kevin Simister, and Joe Thomas.

The team from John Wiley & Sons, Inc. has been utterly fantastic to work with. Lauren Lynch (associate editor) has been a first-rate handler, dealing with all of my eccentricities in a professional manner. Christine Moore's developmental edits have made me look like I can almost write. Lauren Freestone and team did a first-rate job of production. And a special thanks to Matt Holt for positively answering my initial email inquiry exactly ten minutes after I sent it!

I must express deep gratitude to my good friends and past associates at VitalSmarts for partnering with me on the leadership study, giving constant support in this literary undertaking, and never ceasing to show confidence in a successful outcome: Joseph Grenny, Kerry Patterson, Al Switzler, Ron McMillan, Mike Carter, James Allred, Mary Dondiego, Yan Wang, Scott Myler, Andy Shimberg, and Steve Willis.

Heartfelt thanks and recognition go to the Eli Kirk team for early graphic design on the book, and design and construction of our web site.

PART

I

Help Your Company, Help Yourself

What's in It for You?

Because this book is about helping your company, you might be asking, "What's in it for me?" The answer depends on which of the following four career scenarios best describes your situation. If you don't see yourself in any of the four—now or in the future—stop reading.

1. You're one of a small group of people in your company being considered for a highly coveted position that promises more money, opportunity and prestige to whomever gets it. And you want it! What can you do to secure this promotion? Isn't there some way to rise above the competition and become the obvious choice?

2. Rumor has it that another round of layoffs is coming. You've been lucky so far, but you know that luck can't last forever. How can you remove yourself from the list of potential terminations and put yourself at the top of the list of indispensable employees?

3. You're one of millions of people looking for work. The competition is sharp, well educated, and experienced. You need an advantage. What are prospective employers *really* looking for? Can you modify your resume and prepare for interviews in ways that dramatically increase your chances of getting the job you want?

4. You're a leader of a team, department, or company that is made up of wonderful, dedicated employees who know precious little about how to increase the profits of the company. As a leader, you are evaluated based on the performance of your people. How can you engage the collective know-how and full potential of your workforce to positively impact the bottom line?

In the coming pages, you will learn the skills that can dramatically improve your chances of being promoted, avoiding lay-offs, landing a job (if you don't have one), or engaging your people to increase their business value. Are these big promises? While there are no guaranteed outcomes, reading this book over the weekend will prepare you to successfully deal with your current situation. You really can be *Indispensable by Monday*.

You become indispensable at work by bringing in more money than you cost. And you're about to learn how to do just that.

For 30 years, I have had the good fortune of owning or co-owning six companies and learning from some incredibly gifted partners, employees, and customers. Two of those companies were consulting firms. During my 11 years of consulting work, it has been my privilege to assist clients of all sizes in becoming more efficient through interpersonal communication skills, sales expansion, leadership, cost reduction, and survey research. Working with hard dollars as well as soft skills, I've discovered that any business's success or failure depends almost entirely upon individual contributors. Organizations don't succeed, people do. With that conviction, I respectfully write this book for you.

What Does Indispensability Look Like?

I learned about indispensability early through necessity. At the age of 22, I was working my way through college as a machinist manufacturing parts at an aerospace/defense subcontractor firm. I needed the job and the income, and I wanted to perform well. On the first day of this job, I was shown the five machines I would be operating. The trainer told me that my quota of finished parts would be 12 trays of 12 parts each—or144 total parts per day. Though I completed my quota for the first day, I was befuddled by the manufacturing process. The production of each part required me to stand and wait for one machine to finish its automatic, 30-second procedure. Because of the physical arrangement of the machines, I then had to carry the part three machines down the line to perform the next procedure. Next, I carried the part to each of the remaining three machines for completion. I seemed to be wasting a lot of time standing around, watching machines perform automatic functions, and transporting parts back and forth.

On the second day, I came in early and enlisted the help of a maintenance worker to rearrange the machines. The new configuration allowed me to put one part on one machine, and while that part was being processed, start another part on the next machine. As you can imagine, this resulted in a *much* more efficient process; by lunchtime, I had produced 144 completed parts. At the end of the day, there were 288 parts awaiting assembly. I doubled my productivity merely by rearranging the machines.

Over the next couple of weeks, this increase in production caused some interesting challenges. Workers and suppliers who produced the materials I needed had to increase productivity to match mine. The assembly department had to devise ways of increasing their efficiency. But we worked together to come up with solutions that everyone could buy into. As we adjusted, production increased company wide.

One day, as the whole line was humming along at its improved pace, the president of the company came down to the production floor and tapped me on the shoulder. In front of all my coworkers, he told me how happy he was with the improvements, thanked me graciously, shook my oil-soaked hand, and went back up to his office. I felt like a million bucks—only greasier.

Keep in mind that this company's IQ was probably above average. (Did I mention the firm was an aerospace/defense subcontractor?) Yet, despite their genius, they had simply overlooked an opportunity to streamline a process. Other, similarly well-run organizations can miss efficiency opportunities for many reasons. Most commonly, people become comfortable with the established ways of doing things, and they overlook obvious enhancements. Ironically, most improvements are in plain view.[1] Company veterans will often tell you, "This is the way it's done." That may well be true; but the critical approach you will bring to your job on Monday morning is the newcomer's point of view. You will ask "why" of anything and everything in your firm that costs money, takes time (which is money), requires attention (which eats time), and saps energy (which is all you really have to offer). If you do so, you'll find you can perform your job in different and better ways, with improved results.

Will there be times when you will be looked at negatively by coworkers for raising the bar on performance? Maybe. Does that mean you shouldn't do better? Absolutely not, because you can always include them and give them part of the credit for improvements, thereby making your success their success. All it takes is an invitation from you for others to improve upon your ideas and be a part of the implementation.

Employed? Keep the Job You Have . . . Unemployed? Get the Job You Want

In good economic times, the top performers in organizations—or the indispensable employees—regularly receive bonuses, benefits, pay raises, recognition, promotions, and even job offers from other companies. They are always building their resumes and preparing for bigger and brighter things to come. My goal is to help you— through your increased profit contribution skills—enjoy the advantages that are available during such economic upswings.

If your company hits a rough patch financially and is forced to make some cuts in pay, benefits, or personnel, your goal should be to add value to your employer in an effort to increase the chances that you will be seen as a keeper—someone without whom the company would be worse off. When the good times return, you will be well positioned as one of the critical contributors who preserved the company, and you may enjoy the benefits of a company once again in good economic standing.

Should things get *really* tough—as during a wide-scale, deep, and prolonged economic downturn—top performers keep their jobs if the company survives. Unfortunately, even stellar contributors in failing organizations with ugly financial results may not keep their jobs for long, because their individual contributions may not be sufficient to save the company.

If you are currently out of work due to monumental financial upheaval—which could mean that there are lots of people competing for a limited number of available jobs—you'll be able to use the information found here to increase your employability in three ways:

1. *Revamp your resume* as modeled in these pages to highlight your bottom-line profit contributions. You have probably produced some direct financial benefits for past employers, so quantify what you brought to them by properly updating your resume.

2. *Become conversant in the basic language of financial statements* so that you may coherently discuss with job interviewers how you will provide substantial monetary input. (If you are not up to speed on this point, turn to the back of the book and read the section entitled "Everything You Need to Know about Accounting—and It's Not Much.")

3. Before your next interview, *research the company* and determine which of the many profit-enhancing innovations you will be reading about could help your prospective employer.

Bring a couple of the better proposals to the interview and impress the heck out of the interviewer.

These points are broken down further in the following pages.

In order to put your best foot forward in your next job interview, it is critical that your resume properly capture the true value you have created for past employers. I recently had dinner with a relative who told me he had saved his employer some money. Curious about the details, I asked about what he had done, the amount of money saved, and whether his company would continue benefiting in the future from his work. Next, I asked if he had added this accomplishment to his resume. He said he had, so I asked how he had recorded it. His actual resume entry follows:

> *Helped develop innovative procedure to efficiently account and present all extras, time, equipment, material, billing, and history for each of four $1 million + jobs.*

Contrast that with what he had actually done for the company, as expressed here:

> *Developed an innovative process for accurately capturing legitimate billing opportunities formerly overlooked by the company. During the first year of implementation, the process captured $150,000 in revenue that otherwise would have been lost. The recaptured revenue went straight to the bottom line—producing profit comparable to that of a $5 million sale of the company's services.*

As I talked with my relative further, it became clear that he contributed much more than just helping to develop the procedure: The process was actually all his idea! He implemented the process from scratch, and it wouldn't have happened without his persistence.

If all you take from *Indispensable By Monday* is the ability to accurately represent your past accomplishments, that alone is probably worth more than the amount you paid and the time you've spent. My hope is that you take away a whole lot more, such as an awareness of the financial needs of a prospective employer, and a new-found ability to uncover hidden profit. You will be a superior job candidate if you have a documented history of making significant contributions to the bottom line. Combine that history with a working knowledge of the financial objectives of a potential employer and some actual proposals for potential bottom-line contributions (which you will find as you continue reading), and quite simply, you will be a standout!

1,800 Business Leaders Can't Be Wrong: What Your Boss Wants You to Do

In March of 2009, I teamed up with VitalSmarts to create a survey that would establish the value of certain profit-producing behaviors. We asked 1,800 business leaders—primarily in the United States and Canada—how advantageous the core behaviors discussed herein would be if they were exhibited by workers who were being considered for layoffs. Would these behaviors work in favor of employees (keep their jobs), or would they be of no advantage (get laid off)? You probably want to know the outcome of the study before you invest a lot of time becoming skillful in these areas, right? Here's what we found.

Behavior: Regularly Proposes Cost-Cutting Ideas That Work

Of those business leaders, 87.9 percent rated this behavior as being of moderate, substantial, or extreme advantage to a worker being considered for termination. Only 2.9 percent said it would give no advantage to the worker. When asked what percentage of workers in their own companies exhibit this behavior, 8 out of 10 respondents said it was less than 10 percent, on average.

Behavior: Regularly Proposes Revenue-Producing Ideas That Work

Of those business leaders, 88 percent rated this behavior as being of moderate, substantial, or extreme advantage to a worker being considered for termination. Only 4.1 percent said it would give no advantage to the worker. When asked what percentage of workers in their own companies exhibit this behavior, 8 out of 10 respondents said it was less than 8 percent, on average.

Behavior: Streamlines Company Processes to Save Time and Money

Of those business leaders, 94.6 percent rated this behavior as being of moderate, substantial, or extreme advantage to a worker being considered for termination. Only 1.9 percent said it would give no advantage to the worker. When asked what percentage of workers in their own companies exhibit this behavior, 7 out of 10 respondents said it was less than 12 percent, on average.

Behavior: Improves Personal Productivity by Increasing Work Quantity and Quality

Of those business leaders, 93.6 percent rated this behavior as being of moderate, substantial, or extreme advantage to a worker being considered for termination. Only 1.8 percent said it would give no advantage to the worker. When asked what percentage of workers in their own companies exhibit this behavior, 6 out of 10 respondents said it was less than 15 percent, on average.

Behavior: Proposes and/or Implements Procedures to Improve the Cash Flow of the Firm

Finally, of those business leaders, 83.5 percent rated this behavior as being of moderate, substantial, or extreme advantage to a worker being considered for termination. Only 5.8 percent said it would give no advantage to the worker. When asked what percentage of workers in their own companies exhibit this behavior, 9 out of 10 respondents said it was less than 6 percent, on average.

If the absence of valuable behaviors isn't appalling to you, maybe the presence of stupid behaviors will be. We asked about the following political or non-value-added tactics for keeping one's job or getting a promotion. Here they are (and I hope you're not doing any of them):

- Avoid making waves; fit in, live with problems, and avoid speaking up
- Use flattery or favors to ingratiate themselves with the bosses
- Arrive at work before the boss; leave work after the boss
- Generally appear to be busy doing things (often less-important things)
- Make special attempts to be "visible" and claim credit for any good outcome possible

You have no doubt witnessed these—and many other— silly actions on the part of your coworkers, so you might be wondering how often they're happening nationally. Here's the punch line: Our study revealed that the non-value-added tactics are being used by workers twice as frequently as those that add money to the bottom line.

Although leaders can recognize financially sound behaviors as being important to the company and advantageous to their employees, they haven't done the best job of building those skills within the workforce that they lead. Consequently, without the proper skills, knowledge, and ability to enact better strategies, employees have been left on their own to figure out how to make a favorable impression on superiors who are in positions of power. Thus, by default, even smart people lean toward the political—and not the profitable—behaviors.

One final revelation from the study: When asked how beneficial it would be to the company for employees at all levels to have at least a working knowledge of basic accounting concepts such as the Profit and Loss (P&L) Statement, the Balance Sheet, and how the firm makes money, 80.1 percent of respondents answered that it would be of moderate, considerable, or extreme benefit. How many employees actually know this stuff? Seven out of 10 respondents said that less than 13 percent, on average, have this knowledge. You may or may not have this knowledge yourself. If so, read on. If not, go to the section entitled "Everything You Need to Know about Accounting—and It's Not Much" in the back of the book now. It's only a few pages, and you'll need to know the basics before reading any further.

Do You Bring in More Than You Cost?

A basic principle of business is that every company must earn more money than it spends. For that to happen, it would help if all divisions, departments, and subunits of the overall company also earned more money than they spent. That way, each subunit could do its part to contribute to the whole. So, taken to its logical extension, this basic principle would suggest that every *employee* in the company must also be profitable. If you had a personal P&L Statement that depicted the value you bring to your employer and the amount you cost your employer taped to your back, what do you suppose it would look like? Do you generate more revenue for the company than you cost as an employee?

When you were hired, the management of your company decided that your position was critical to realize more revenue than expenses. Businesses don't hire people and carry the attendant expense just for fun. You were asked to join the organization because somebody concluded that your position, generally, and you, specifically, would bring in more value than cost. Were they right? You might think so; but would the key decision makers agree? Every manager has a list of the strong and weak people under them. At times, this value-added equation is official; sometimes, it is unofficial. Sometimes, it is mental, and sometimes, it's written out. But it is always there. The decision to create your position—and fill it with you—was made using this very thought process.

You may be under the impression that your hiring could not have been based on such a cold calculation. Rather, your boss hired you because you are good with people, a team player, or have a great resume. You are most likely correct in that reasoning. You probably *were* hired because of your ability to work and play well with others. However, management assumed that those interpersonal skills would translate into added value or profit to the company. Likewise, your past experience almost certainly *was* a factor in your company offering you a job, because your boss thought that your experience would add more value than someone with a thinner resume.

So, let's evaluate your personal P&L Statement to quantify what you're bringing to the company and what you're taking away. It's important to see a net positive impact, because just as no company can exist for long without profit, no employee can expect to remain employed for long without making a net positive contribution. Even if you are currently bringing the value to your employer that he or she hoped for at your hiring, indispensability comes from adding more value than he or she expected.

If your job can be directly linked to the generation of revenue—like sales, sales support, or hourly billing—it's fairly easy for you to calculate what you bring to the company. For those of you not in one of these positions, you may wonder how you can calculate your value to the company. Don't despair! You can contribute to the company's bottom line, even if you have never seen the sales department or billed a client for a single minute of your time.

> *"The company just can't afford to keep you on the payroll any longer."*
>
> **Translation:**
> *"We ran the numbers, and you cost more than your financial contribution."*
>
> **Solution:**
> *Start contributing more than you cost!*

Employees bring both tangible assets (actual dollars) and intangible assets (your personal abilities to create value and find dollars); so, both direct revenue generators (salespeople and hourly billers) and all other employees can contribute in important financial ways to the company. The next section tells you how to calculate those contributions.

Personal P&L Statement for Direct Revenue Generators

Let's start with those directly involved with sales. Build your personal P&L Statement by filling in the blanks in the form

Personal P&L Direct Revenue Generator

Revenue You Bring to Your Company

Gross sales (made by you) of the company's products/services _____

Gross Sales on which you worked in essential support _____

Gross Revenue from Hours Billed _____

*Other Revenue:*_____ _____

_____

What You Cost Your Company

Annual compensation (salary or hourly)

Commission _____

Annual Bonus _____

Benefits (Medical/Dental/Retirement) _____

Auto Allowance _____

Space you occupy at $X/sq. ft. _____

Mistakes/rework you caused _____

Management time you require at $X/hr _____

*Other costs:*_____ _____

_____ _____

Your Estimated Net Profit (Loss) to Your Company _____

Figure 1.1

found in Figure 1.1. Don't worry about getting the numbers exactly right; estimates are fine for now. Use a 12-month period as your time frame.

While the sales team receives a lot of the kudos within the organization, you should know that there are profitable sales and not-so-profitable sales. For example, if the company's typical net-profit margin on a sale is 5 percent, and if a salesperson discounts the normal sales price by 6 percent in order to close a deal, then that sales person isn't producing any net value. Instead, they have actually produced a net loss on that sale. This practice may occasionally be advantageous during slow times when the company needs cash flow; however, it is not sustainable. Another costly mistake that inadequate sales people resort to is overpromising certain features or committing their organizations to unreasonably short delivery times. These deals, even when sold at full price, can also produce net losses when the costs associated with rushed delivery and maintenance exceed the typical profit margin.

Needless to say, a good sales force that understands the basics of accounting and profit generation is invaluable to any organization. Accordingly, if you're a solid sales rep, your personal P&L Statement is practically bulletproof. Even better, there are methods for sales professionals to create astounding additional value for their employers—beyond basic sales quotas—due to the direct contact they have with customers. These contributions are explored in a later section.

Nonsales Personal P&L Statement

If you are currently not in sales, before you put in your request for a transfer to the sales department, you should know that in most cases, the lion's share of sales compensation is tied directly to performance: No sales, no pay. It's a tough career, where only the winners survive, and the pressure to perform is relentless.

If you are not in sales and you don't bill clients directly for your time, is the concept of indispensability completely out of reach for you? Not by a long shot! The question we want to answer is whether your personal P&L results in a net profit or loss. Let's look at what your P&L could—and should—include.

Regardless of whether you are a direct revenue generator, such as a salesperson or an hourly biller, or a secretary in the accounting department, if you are not now contributing in the following cost-cutting and revenue-increasing categories, you can be—and soon. By exploring each category, you can discover how to add indispensable value to your organization. (Of course, sales reps can also engage in any and all of the profit-producing opportunities shown in this P&L, and nonsales employees often participate in critical, sales-related activities. The distinction between sales and nonsales P&Ls has been emphasized only to put an end to the myth that salespeople are the only ones who have opportunities to create profit for the company.) See the Nonsales Personal P&L Statement in Figure 1.2.

Non-Sales Personal P&L Statement

Revenue or Cost Savings You Bring to Your Company
Cost saving initiatives _____
New revenue generated from existing customers _____
Revenue generation from refunds and rebates _____
Process improvement measures (efficiencies) _____
Mistakes/rework/at-risk revenue you rescued _____
Customers you salvaged after mistakes by your company _____
Quantity and quality improvements in your own job _____
Unofficial encounters with customers _____
Suppliers and customers with whom you shared profit increases _____
Cash flow improvements _____
Improvements in your company's value proposition to customers _____
Improvements in your own value proposition to your company _____
Other Revenue _____

What You Cost Your Company
Annual compensation (salary or hourly) _____
Annual bonus _____
Benefits _____
Auto allowance _____
Space you occupy at $X/sq. ft. _____
Management time you require at $X/hr _____
Mistakes/rework you caused _____
*Other costs:*_____ _____
_____ _____

Your Estimated Net Profit (Loss) to Your Company _____

Figure 1.2

All Dollars Are Not Created Equal: How to Find the Most Valuable Ones

Every employee should increase his or her personal P&L by uncovering hidden and unexpected dollars. You may think that any new dollar is of equal value to your company. This is not so. The dollars you can produce by finding hidden revenue or unexpected cost reductions are much more valuable to your company than the top-line dollars produced through ordinary sales. Found—or unexpected—dollars are added directly to bottom-line profit, while typical sales dollars are loaded with overhead such as commission, cost of goods sold, and general and administrative expenses. In other words: You are bringing in one-hundred-cent dollars, while the sales staff is bringing in seven-cent dollars (assuming that the company has a net-profit margin of 7 percent). If a salesperson makes quota, it's expected; but if you discover hidden money, it's a windfall.

To understand the power of this concept, look at Figure 1.3. Here, you can see what $25,000 produced by you would be worth to the company in equivalent sales dollars. Find your company's profit margin to determine the amount of sales needed to produce $25,000 in profit on the company's P&L. Keep in mind that we are talking about the company's net profit, not gross revenue.

You can tell by looking at the table that the narrower the profit margin, the more valuable your contribution. If your company is losing money right now—meaning that there is no profit margin because the bottom line of its P&L is negative—then *any* revenue or unexpected dollars you produce will be extremely valuable, because every dollar will bring the company closer to the sustainable state of profit. In a loss situation, it is imperative to return to profitability as quickly as possible; and you will be a superstar if you can help that effort.

Bottom-Line Profit	Profit Margin	Equivalent Sales
$25,000	1%	$2,500,000
$25,000	2%	$1,250,000
$25,000	3%	$833,333
$25,000	4%	$625,000
$25,000	5%	$500,000
$25,000	6%	$416,667
$25,000	7%	$357,143
$25,000	8%	$312,500
$25,000	9%	$277,778
$25,000	10%	$250,000
$25,000	11%	$227,273
$25,000	12%	$208,333
$25,000	13%	$192,308
$25,000	14%	$178,571
$25,000	15%	$166,667
$25,000	16%	$156,250
$25,000	17%	$147,059
$25,000	18%	$138,889
$25,000	19%	$131,579
$25,000	20%	$125,000

Figure 1.3

The Resume That Speaks Volumes: Capture Your Contributions

As you implement the ideas you're learning, you'll need to document your indispensability. If you are unemployed, you will want to bolster your resume by properly capturing past financial contributions. You are about to learn how to do just that. If you are employed, you will want to keep your resume current for performance reviews and to be considered for promotions. Either way, the resume is where you will want to update and store your accomplishments. And if written correctly, your resume will forever capture and showcase the profit contributions that an employer can't live without. Assume that your company operates with a net-profit margin of 7 percent, and you use the knowledge in this book to create unexpected profit of $25,000 added to the bottom line. You should chronicle your financial indispensability in the following manner:

Improved the company's shipping process by removing unnecessary steps, resulting in a $25,000 annual profit contribution. The profit from this improvement was equal to the profit from $357,143 in annual sales revenue, or $1,785,715 in total sales equivalency over five years.

In this example, we used the random amount of $25,000. You may be concerned that you won't be able to create that much value. On the other hand, you may already know of ways to save or create that much—or even far more—for your company. No matter your present confidence level, my commitment to you is to transfer the skills, knowledge, and tools to accomplish all that you are able. At the end of the day, you will probably surprise yourself.

Just for kicks, let's create two new resume entries representing $1,000 and $100,000 profit contributions. Again, the calculations assume a company net profit of 7 percent.

For the Faint of Heart

Improved the company's shipping process by removing unnecessary steps, resulting in a $1,000 annual profit contribution. The profit from this improvement was equal to the profit from $14,286 in annual sales revenue, or $71,429 in total sales equivalency over five years.

For the Overachiever

Improved the company's shipping process by removing unnecessary steps, resulting in a $100,000 annual profit contribution. The profit from this improvement was equal to the profit from $1,428,571 in annual sales revenue, or $7,142,857 in total sales equivalency over five years.

Learn the simple math behind the sales-equivalency calculation, and you will be able to quickly determine the sales value of any cost reduction you are considering:

$$\text{Amount of Savings } (\$25,000) \div \text{Profit Margin } (0.07)$$
$$= \text{Sales Equivalent } (\$357,143)$$

$$\$25,000 \div 0.07 = \$357,143$$

If you don't want to deal with the math, you can simply input your idea into the Profit Proposal Generator (PPG) at www.indispensablebymonday.com, and the tool will calculate sales equivalency and many other functions for you. This free service allows you to produce profit proposals of exceptional quality, even though you may not have formal financial training.

Because your ideas must be implemented in order to legitimately make their way to your resume, it is extremely important to format and analyze your proposals professionally. The right analysis and presentation will greatly increase the chances of implementation. The PPG was created for this purpose. As you move into the next section, you will discover how key the PPG tool can be in formatting, vetting, and presenting your profit ideas—making them resonate with decision makers in your organization.

Death of the Suggestion Box: May It Rest in Pieces

We've all seen it: that pitiful, forlorn, beat-up thing that gathers dust on the outside while remaining empty on the inside. The hinges on the lid are mostly broken, due not to overuse but instead to cheap construction. After all, who wants to put a lot of money into a suggestion box? For that matter, who wants to put a *suggestion* into a suggestion box? My favorite dysfunctional part is the tiny slot cut into the lid. To actually use the antiquated thing, one must either write on a tiny piece of paper or use regular-sized paper and then fold and fold and fold. It was like passing notes to Cathy Rissi this way in kindergarten. I didn't know how to write, so it was just as well that the bulk of the time spent on our love-note interaction was me folding and her unfolding. Even if I could have written something, she couldn't read, so the folding/unfolding was fine.

Anyway, let's say you get the suggestion written and in the box. What next? How do you know it will get picked up? They have locks on those things, you know. It's not like you can come into work early the next morning and open the box to see if it's been emptied. I guess if the slot in the lid is big enough, you could put some already-chewed gum on the end of a pencil and poke it in. If it comes out empty, you're in good shape, but if you pull out your original suggestion, maybe you could jot down another suggestion on the reverse side that reads, "I suggest you empty this box once a day." Of course, if you come back the next day with more gum and another pencil and find they still haven't emptied the box, then I'm fresh out of suggestions for you. (Grade school was fun, wasn't it?)

A Better Way

Is it just me, or is this whole box thing a bit juvenile—not to mention outdated? The suggestion box got its illustrious start over 200 years ago.[2] The original motivation behind its invention was to offer an anonymous method to voice grievances and offer ideas that might not sit well with powerful and intimidating superiors. This forum was chosen in order to take away any fear of reprisal and thereby invite broad-based, free-flowing participation.

As you might expect, the old-fashioned box is still around in some companies. You may even have one next to your water cooler. You'll find them most frequently in manufacturing settings where computers are scarce. The box has had its ups and downs over the years but has clearly become a relic that probably gathers as many gripes and complaints as profit-producing ideas.

The Internet and a host of software development companies have improved things quite a bit in the last 12 to 15 years. We are now on generation three of idea-management programs, so things are moving in the right direction from a technology standpoint. Ideas are being tracked and implemented in much more expeditious and orderly ways today. Some programs are even helping with creative idea generation at the front end of innovation management. This can increase both the quantity and quality of profit-enhancement initiatives. Still, one of the main complaints about enterprise-wide innovation efforts is that employees are offering too many ideas that are just plain bad. Let's explore what makes a proposal unacceptable:

A Bad Proposal

- Costs too much to implement; the payback time is too long
- Requires too much analysis to determine its feasibility
- Doesn't yield any substantial benefit because it's too small
- Contains personal gripes instead of constructive business improvements
- Doesn't focus on any critical issues
- Cuts into the meat of strategy, not just the fat of inefficiency
- Hinders the organization's ability to serve customers
- Doesn't take into account the company's economic situation
- Violates the company's or the workforce's code of ethics
- Is discriminatory
- Is illegal

The list could go on, but the main point is this: You should evaluate proposals *before* they are scrutinized by your firm's decision makers. Certainly, you want to be known as the person who offers solid, educated, workable improvements in a professional format (with no folding.) Notice the contrast between the following two submissions illustrated in Figures 1.4 and 1.5 for the same profit proposal.

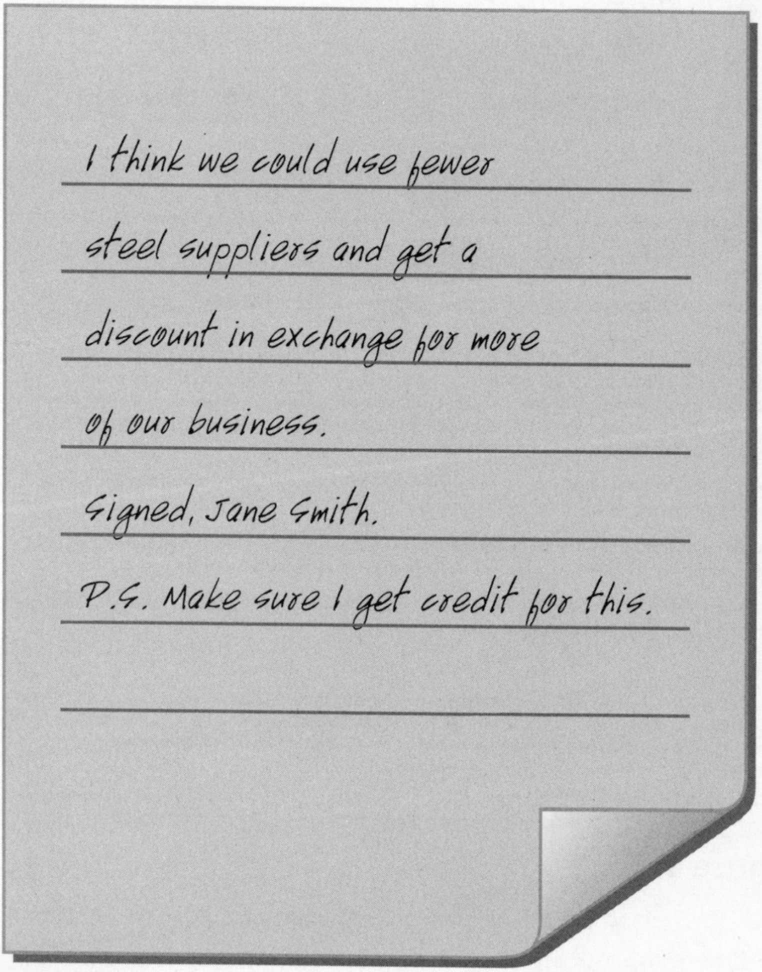

I think we could use fewer

steel suppliers and get a

discount in exchange for more

of our business.

Signed, Jane Smith.

P.S. Make sure I get credit for this.

Figure 1.4

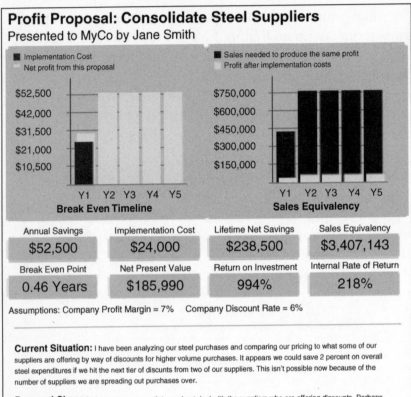

Profit Proposal: Consolidate Steel Suppliers
Presented to MyCo by Jane Smith

■ Implementation Cost
 Net profit from this proposal

■ Sales needed to produce the same profit
 Profit after implementation costs

Break Even Timeline — Y1 Y2 Y3 Y4 Y5 ($52,500 / $42,000 / $31,500 / $21,000 / $10,500)

Sales Equivalency — Y1 Y2 Y3 Y4 Y5 ($750,000 / $600,000 / $450,000 / $300,000 / $150,000)

Annual Savings	Implementation Cost	Lifetime Net Savings	Sales Equivalency
$52,500	$24,000	$238,500	$3,407,143

Break Even Point	Net Present Value	Return on Investment	Internal Rate of Return
0.46 Years	$185,990	994%	218%

Assumptions: Company Profit Margin = 7%   Company Discount Rate = 6%

Current Situation: I have been analyzing our steel purchases and comparing our pricing to what some of our suppliers are offering by way of discounts for higher volume purchases. It appears we could save 2 percent on overall steel expenditures if we hit the next tier of discunts from two of our suppliers. This isn't possible now because of the number of suppliers we are spreading out purchases over.

Proposal Change: I propose we negotiate our best deal with the suppliers who are offering discounts. Perhaps we can get 3 percent if we play it right.

Benefits of Proposal: This can be implemented with reasonable transition costs. Attached is my analysis of the benefits of this change. You will notice that the total profit increase we would achieve is $52,500 annually.

Barriers to Implementation: It will take substantial staff time to negotiate this change. We will also need to deal with existing purchase orders in the pipeline.

Figure 1.5

The professional quality of your proposals is critical in your pursuit of indispensability. The PPG tool is user friendly, requires no financial expertise, and is free. (Be careful about how hard you push for personal recognition in the proposal itself, because it is more professional to be low key about it at this stage. Your resume is the place to toot your own horn. The fact that your proposal is from you will be well documented when you use this tool. Just be sure to submit all proposals to your company electronically, and you're covered.)

If you have a cost-cutting or revenue-increasing idea, go to www.indispensablebymonday.com and try it out now. If you do not have any ideas yet, you are about to find some in Part 2, which starts now. Fasten your financial seat belt!

PART

Pull Money out of Thin Air

Creating Unexpected Profit Is Always Your Best Strategy

In 1896, the son of a farmer and grandson of a poor, Irish immigrant, Henry Ford created his quadricycle. He produced his first working engine from nothing but scrap. Collecting a hand-wheel from an old lathe and a piece of discarded pipe, he fashioned a flywheel and cylinder. A piece of fiber with a wire through its center acted as a spark plug. Where no value seemed to exist, Henry Ford's first automobile was born.[3]

Here in Part 2, I'll reveal 14 profit sources you can draw from to add monetary value to your company's bottom line. Like Henry Ford, you'll soon be creating something from nothing. You'll be pulling money out of thin air.

WARNING! Do not attempt to read all of Part 2 at one time. This section contains a high concentration of profit enhancing ideas. You will find a way to increase profits for your company in any 5 of the next 100 pages. Choose one of the following 14 profit source chapters, read until you discover a profit idea that you can apply to your company, then use the Profit Proposal Generator to document the financial impact. Submit the proposal, read another 5 pages, create and submit another proposal. Start on Monday; repeat until promoted.

Yes, There Are Still Costs to Be Cut

You might think that management has saved all that it possibly can by cutting costs. Maybe the workforce in your company has recently organized an extensive cost-reduction effort, and although you've racked your brain, you cannot come up with any ideas for saving any *more* money. You may be right; there may be nothing left. It could be that all of the low-hanging fruit has been harvested, and all that remains are small cuts that won't yield much or would be too expensive to implement. If so, don't worry. Cost cutting is only one of many categories of profit enhancement you will learn about here. However, consider this: If no one is expecting more dollars from cost reductions and you *do* come up with substantial savings, then you will be regarded as having super powers. So, let's figure out a way to make that happen.

Believe it or not, there is almost *always* significant value to be found in the expense section of any company's Profit and Loss Statement. And while the P&L is a good map to get you started in your hunt for savings, you also need to look around and ask a lot of questions in order to find these hidden dollars. Expenses that are subject to reduction are often more recognizable in the real world than they are on a financial report. For example, the P&L might show expenditures for the company's real estate (taxes, insurance, maintenance, etc.), but until you talk with a few neighboring real estate owners, you won't discover that they have recently negotiated with the county tax commission and successfully petitioned for a reduction in property taxes. If they have done it, your company can, too. This opportunity would not show up on the P&L, but you could uncover it through an active, physical search. Think like a newcomer and explore all options that could lead to better ways of getting what the company needs for less money.

Figure 2.1 is a typical list of expenses taken from the expense section of a P&L Statement. Your company's P&L will vary from this example, but this will get us started.

Our quest in reducing company costs begins with real estate and related property expenses. Then, we'll discuss slashing and saving in other categories.

Selling Expense

Advertising
Sales Salary
Sales Commissions
Referral Fees

Employee Expense

Hourly Labor
Salary Labor
Payroll Tax
Health Benefits
Other Benefits

Insurance & Professional Fees

Property Insurance
Key Leader Insurance
Multi Peril Insurance
Legal
Accounting

Office Expense

Vehicles
Bank Fees
Delivery Service
Meals & Entertainment
Telephone
Internet
Utilities
Rent
Equipment Leases
Repair and Maintenance
Supplies

Major Suppliers *(Raw Materials, and Components)*

Figure 2.1

Real Estate: A Rich Source of Hidden (and Reducible) Costs

Real estate expenses are somewhat hidden. They are not typically represented as one comprehensive line item on a financial report; however, they consume a tremendous amount of company resources. This is, therefore, one of the richest categories for discovering hidden profits. Owning real estate is an expensive proposition. When a company constructs or buys a building, it commits to paying a long list of unrelenting expenses that can almost always be reduced. Because virtually all real estate-related expenses repeat—and most often increase—annually for the life of the building, reducing expenses here is more valuable than producing a one-time cost reduction elsewhere in your company.

At this juncture, I should tell you that there will be times when you find something that is too small to get excited about. Yet, you should always explore the long-term value of any repeating cost-saving initiative that you discover. Multiple locations offer an even larger compounding effect to any savings you find. If your company owns dozens or even hundreds of properties, you only need to find one small cost reduction (multiplied by the number of sites to which it can be applied) to create a huge contribution to the bottom line. As you learn about the many ways your company is spending money on real estate, you should find many more occasions for cost cutting.

Sewer Savings

If possible, get a detailed copy of your company's P&L, and look in the expense section at the amount of money spent on sewer, water, garbage, gas, electricity, and phones. You will be surprised at how much is spent on these services. Wherever the company spends large amounts of money, there is a greater likelihood that it may be able to save some as well. Companies often assume that these expenses simply must be paid and fail to question why and for what they are being billed. Here's how I racked up substantial savings in this arena.

My firm was engaged by a Fortune 500 company to help increase profits. The client had just completed an extensive, company-wide cost-cutting effort. Sound familiar? Frankly, the CFO didn't expect us to find any inefficient spending, given the thorough work that had already been done. But we did. Among other savings, we produced a reduction in their sewer bill, of all things, in the amount of $1,400. Doesn't sound like much, does it? At first glance, $1,400 would fit into the too-small-to-get-excited-about category; however, this was $1,400 *per month*. That's $16,800 per year and $168,000 over 10 years. Given the 5 percent profit margin of our client, the profit was equivalent to that of $3.36 million in sales over 10 years.

Would you like to know how we created this cost reduction—and possibly even replicate it in your company? Well, you must first understand the process. The city or county installs a water meter to measure the amount of clean, drinkable water supplied to your place of business. Your company also receives a monthly bill for sewer services. Here's the thing: The sewer bill is calculated based on water consumption. In other words, the city or county assumes, for billing purposes, that the number of gallons of water coming into your business through the water meter is the same number of gallons that gets flushed down toilets, drained from sinks, and used in production processes—all of which goes into the public sewer system.

But what if some of the metered water doesn't go into the public sewer system? When your employer turns on the sprinklers to water the shrubs, trees, and grass outside, where does *that* water go? It does not go into the sewer system. Some of it evaporates into the atmosphere, some sinks into the ground, and some runs into the storm drain system. So, if you can calculate the amount of water consumed for landscaping rather than channeled into the sewer, you may request that the sewer utility refrain from billing your company that amount of the sewer charge. All you have to do is count the sprinkler heads, read the flow capacity (in gallons per minute) on each one, and determine the total time of operation of each sprinkler head. This calculation tells you how many gallons did *not* drain into the sewer system during the year, and that is the number of gallons for which your company is being overcharged on its sewer bill. Here are some details you should keep in mind as you pursue this cost-saving strategy:

1. It's important to quantify an annual amount of water, because warmer months require more watering than colder months. A calculation based on one month alone will not be accurate and will therefore be subject to dispute.

2. You must be sure the sprinkler system is in fact using culinary water and not irrigation water. If it's irrigation water, there is no savings opportunity.

3. Check the law in your state. The Public Utilities Commission (PUC, alternately called the PSC or Public Service Commission in some states) is the governing body that establishes the laws regarding utility billing calculations and administration. Consult the PUC's (or PSC's) statutes to verify that your company can apply for this billing reduction.

Once you have determined the extent to which your company is being overcharged—and have ensured that items 1 through 3 are in line—it is a simple matter of making a written request to the billing entity to correct this oversight in all future bills. Include pertinent documentation with this correspondence. If your company owns multiple buildings with large landscaped areas, this may be a substantial savings opportunity for you.

Here's another chance for sewer savings. Public works departments within cities and counties charge varying fees for sewer services, depending on a customer's industry. Some industries use chemicals and other toxins in their business processes and are therefore charged more for sewer treatment services than other, less-polluting industries. Can you guess what industry is generally charged the most per gallon of waste water due to the pollutants it contains? Mortuaries. Find out what the industry classification is for your company's sewer billing calculations. Is it accurate? Was it accurate at one time but has since been changed? Is there another billing class that would be more accurate and less expensive? If so, you have just discovered another cost reduction. A letter requesting the reclassification and a reduction in future billing should be all it takes.

Utilities Savings

Okay, let's climb out of the sewer but stay in utilities for now. I like the area of utilities when it comes to cost-reduction efforts, because people in your organization, including upper management, generally don't understand the complexities of utility charges. Who really does? Well, you can—with a little work. Go to the various utility offices with a copy of your company's bills in hand, and become educated as to why you are on a particular billing program. Occasionally, there are cheaper alternatives—such as industry classifications for sewer users—that are not automatically offered without a customer request. Ask questions, and understand every charge. Inaccuracies and mistakes are commonplace. You may find you are being charged for services that you are not receiving, or you may be receiving (and paying for) services you don't need.

With regard to your electric bill, pay close attention to the peak demand charge, which may play a big role in the overall cost. Find out what lowering the peak demand would do to the cost, and then work on ways to lower the peak power requirement by modifying your company's operations. Because every company is unique in this regard, it wouldn't help to get into specifics on the topic of electricity consumption. This information is intended to point you in the right direction.

An alternative to exploring utility cost savings internally is to recommend that the company hire a utility consultant to perform audits and seek out all available cost reductions. Such consultants generally work on a contingency fee basis and cost nothing if they find nothing. If you have the inclination, you can do some investigation on your own before hiring a consultant.

I have provided you with the preceding information as though you are the person to implement these cost-reduction ideas. Of course, this probably will not be the case in large or mid-sized organizations, where your proposal will move up the ladder and land on someone's desk for evaluation, and passing that hurdle, be implemented. However, if you work in a small company and you desire to, you may get the chance to personally do some of this research and legwork. If you do, it can be gratifying; it can even be done on lunch breaks or before or after work (although most employers would be thrilled to have you save them money during your normal working time). Just be careful that your usual responsibilities are not hindered by these types of activities without the blessing of management.

Property Taxes

Tax rates should be reviewed every couple of years, especially any time local property values go down. You must petition the county tax commission for a reduction. The commission accepts and reviews petitions once a year. They may send out written notice of when the review occurs, or you may call to determine the date. You can prepare to challenge the amount of tax you pay by obtaining an appraisal and comparing it to the commission's tax valuation. You must then present your findings to the commission. If you're not comfortable with this process, enlist the help of a qualified property tax consulting firm, which would be paid a percentage of any reduction they are able to obtain.

Property Insurance

You may reduce costs by ensuring that your company has purchased the correct type of insurance. Fire insurance rates are based on the construction of the building (steel frame or wood frame), the contents stored in the building (flammable or nonflammable), and the use of the building (high- or low-fire-risk operation). Did your company buy the coverage that's currently in place at a time when the stored materials or the business operations were different than they are today? If that's the case, then a price reduction may be possible. Also, different insurance companies specialize in underwriting different industries. These distinctions sometimes create wide variations in premium calculations. Your company should check with several providers to get the best price from the best-fitting insurance provider.

Additional cost-reducing policy changes are equally as simple. Liability insurance costs can often be diminished by raising the deductable payment. And given the level of competition in the insurance industry, a simple request for a price reduction from your existing insurance company is sometimes granted. Your request will bear more consideration if your company has a good track record of timely payments and no claims made on the policy for the past three years.

Cleaning

It is interesting that an area as mundane as cleaning can produce truly considerable savings. One janitor found profit as he carefully considered where to save his company money. He changed cleaning solutions, which saved him a small amount of money per year in one building. The idea transferred company wide to all 600 locations. Not many janitors have a resume that reads like this:

My research indicated a less-expensive cleaning product would meet our needs. Switching products saved over $50 per year for each of the company's 600 locations. Total annual savings was $30,000 and will continue in the future. Profit in one year from this change was equal to the net profit from $428,571 in regular company sales.

Maintenance

All buildings and the contents therein must be maintained. Companies would save a small fortune if buildings and their content didn't wear out, get damaged, or become obsolete; however, they do. Building contents are commonly referred to as furniture, fixtures, and equipment (FF&E) and are shown as assets on your company's Balance Sheet. Another category of building contents would be materials, either in the form of goods used to make product or inventory of finished product ready for delivery. Inventory is also a Balance Sheet asset category, as is real estate itself. Buildings—and all the stuff inside them—require never-ending effort and money to maintain. While buildings and the contents therein are Balance Sheet assets, the cost of maintaining them is accounted for in the P&L. Maintenance expenses, in all their varieties, represent a continual and substantial flow of money that you can reduce. Consider the following possibilities.

Building maintenance includes regular maintenance and periodic needed repairs or replacement in these areas:

- Landscaping
- Parking lot surface (cleaning, resurfacing, striping, and snow removal)
- Roof and other building exterior surfaces
- Flooring and interior surfaces
- Building structure
- Heating, ventilation, and air conditioning (HVAC)

As you look at this partial list and observe how your company is dealing with these expenses, question what could be done differently to reduce costs. Can workers within the company take over some of these maintenance responsibilities as a part of their normal job description? Can you recommend extending the time until new carpet is installed in certain areas of the building? Are there materials for flooring, roofing, or window tinting that will have a longer life for a better price than that which would normally be purchased? This is a boring expense category that has probably been ignored for years; so, use a little imagination and find a lot of savings. Check out this resume entry:

Commissioned a free study by the local electric company of summertime thermal loading on my employer's buildings. In order to reduce cooling costs, we transplanted mature shade trees from company grounds to new sunny-side locations next to a number of buildings in order to provide optimal shade during warm days of the year. This initiative resulted in saving the company over $2,000 annually. Net profit from this idea was equal to that of $28,571 in company sales. This benefit will recur annually, yielding a sales equivalency of $142,857 over the next five years.

Furniture, Fixtures, and Equipment

As a category, furniture, fixtures and equipment (FF&E) is self-explanatory. In manufacturing, the main focus should be on equipment—especially that which is used to manufacture end-user products. Maintenance costs can run high on expensive equipment; much more so in crisis situations. Here's a common scenario: An expensive machine is not properly maintained as it should be. When a breakdown occurs, it always seems to be at the most critical time, and everyone scrambles to get the equipment up and running again *now*—whatever the cost! Later, when we look back and see the P&L on our operations, we wonder what the heck we were thinking.

What can you do to ensure the continuous, efficient, and lowest cost operation of key equipment in your company? Are the manufacturer's maintenance protocols being followed exactly? An ounce of prevention really can be worth a pound of cure when you're talking about a $2 million piece of equipment. Do you understand the terms of warranties, and are you following those terms to the letter, so as not to void them? Become indispensable by being one of the few in your organization who really understands the details of key equipment maintenance and downtime prevention. A simple suggestion could go a long way on your resume:

Suggested that the company compile a notebook of all warranties and maintenance schedules for every applicable piece of equipment company wide. Copies of this binder were distributed to each maintenance worker and supervisor, with specific servicing responsibilities assigned in a more organized way than had been done before. All warranty parts and services were *paid for and provided by our suppliers, and no warranties were voided due to unauthorized service by our staff. The result was a lowering of unscheduled downtime and crisis maintenance, for a total first-year savings of $17,500, which was the same profit as producing $250,000 in sales for the company. Additionally, due to increased efficiencies, all production quotas and custom orders were filled on schedule for the first time in two years, adding $375,000 to the company's revenue that year, with no overtime expenses.*

If you work in a service company and don't manufacture a product, you can still look for ways to extend the life of furniture, fixtures, and equipment by keeping desks, computers, filing cabinets, and conference tables clean, protected, and well maintained. Perhaps you are handy or know someone in the company who is and can quickly repair certain items rather than have the company pay to replace them. What thoughts do you have to keep that finicky copier running properly? Be the one who really cares about how well the FF&E is performing for everyone in the office, and add a little something to your resume in the process:

After expressing my company's dissatisfaction with the unreliable performance of our copier, I negotiated an additional year of upgraded maintenance from our office equipment provider. The machine performed well with the increased attention, and we were able to defer a $16,000 purchase of a new copier until the following budget year.

Major Suppliers (Raw Materials and Components)

Raw Materials

Depending on the business in question, raw materials often must be protected from the elements and kept fresh and undamaged while in transit to your company or while stored there. If damage is the fault of the supplier, seek a credit or discount against their bill. Requesting compensation where appropriate is an opportunity for you to be a real bulldog for your employer. Nobody wants to take the blame for damaged goods, but you should hold the proper party fully responsible. If you have a storage yard or warehouse where raw materials are kept, find out whether the storage and retrieval methods are damaging expensive inventory. There are many opportunities for materials to get damaged in storage or transit. For instance, forklift operators navigating narrow aisles can beat the living daylights out of stored stock. Are inventory managers using the newest materials for production rather than the oldest? This can cause unnecessary aging or expiration of inventory. Find out how much money is regularly lost by your company due to damage, spoilage, shrinkage (theft), or obsolescence, and look for ways to reduce those losses:

Organized the storage bays so that our inventory of packaged cement could be moved back under the overhead shelter an additional 20 feet. This eliminated the occasional situation where cement would be ruined during rainstorms throughout the year. Annual savings of $3,000 was equivalent in profit to $42,857 in top-line sales revenue.

Finished Products (or Services)

Completed work embodies all of the time, effort, and money spent in preparing to convert your company's product or service into cash. Look for costs that can reasonably be taken out of the quality assurance process, packaging, tracking, or loading procedures, while protecting the product from damage or theft. If a service has been rendered to a company and not billed—or billed and not collected—you are losing money with each passing day. If you have a product that is ready to ship, get it shipped now. Where appropriate, bill the client for shipping charges and any insurance your customer requests or your company deems necessary. Often, as a policy, these charges will be paid by your company. If so, ask why, and look at ways to include these charges in the client billing. If your company normally covers shipping and insurance, contact customers just before shipment and ask if they have a need to get the product sooner than your standard delivery time. If the answer is yes, inform them that they will need to pay shipping. Often, customers will have an urgent need for your product and may be willing to cover a higher-priority shipping charge to expedite its delivery:

Established a new system for contacting customers to let them know their orders were ready to ship. During each customer contact, a simple option was offered regarding shipping preference: They could either get three-day shipping for free or a higher-priority delivery service, which they would pay for. Customers chose to pay for faster delivery 20 percent of the time, reducing our shipping costs by $12,500 per year. This is the same amount of profit produced by $178,571 in product sales. An unexpected benefit of this innovation was the enhanced service our customers felt they were receiving due to the added contact, as at times, we updated shipping addresses and other incorrect customer information.

Cutting any of these materials and property-related expenses adds up over the term of your employment. Big savings means real indispensability.

Other Costs

Using the framework of the expense section of a common P&L, here are some proven cost-cutting methods you may wish to propose in your company:

Advertising

1. Track which advertising efforts are successful and which are not, and cut the losers.

2. Have the supplier or manufacturer of one of your products (or raw materials) pay for part of your advertising costs. They have a vested interest in you selling their product. This practice is known as cooperative advertising, and it's done every day.

Sales Compensation/Referral Fees

1. Shift more sales compensation from base pay (fixed cost, no matter how much or little is sold) to commission (paid only on actual sales). This will lower compensation expenses if sales slow down.

2. Modify referral-fee agreements so that full fees are paid on the first deal, with a graduated reduction for subsequent transactions.

Hourly Labor

1. Develop a plan to keep turnover and new-hire training costs low.

2. Establish a probation period for new employees before benefits begin. Also, begin paying a full hourly rate only after job proficiency is reached.

3. Offer special recognition or incentives for money-saving achievements, such as the most days without an accident or the least sick days taken in a certain time period.

4. Shift as many workers as possible to direct deposit instead of paper paychecks.

5. Reserve pay raises and bonuses for top performers only.

Bank Fees

1. In most cases, bank fees can be negotiated down to zero.

2. While at the bank, establish a sweep account that automatically puts excess cash into the highest possible interest rate account. (By the way, this is a revenue-enhancing strategy, but it seemed convenient to insert here).

Look through the other categories of the P&L, and be tenaciously creative about ways to find dollars. Enter your ideas into the Profit Proposal Generator at www.indispensablebymonday .com, and submit your profit proposals with pride.

Ansoff Revisited—How to Harvest More Money from Customers

2 Profit Source

Many organizations begin and end their profit improvement efforts by attempting to reduce costs and seem to forget the other half of their P&L Statements. A P&L contains income (revenue) as well as expenses. Obviously, an organization that reduces expenses *and* increases revenue will benefit from a healthier bottom line. So, why is it that cost reduction alone gets most of the attention in the quest for profit? The answer probably lies within the following partially accurate assumptions:

1. Revenue is handled by sales and marketing.

2. It's easy to cut costs, because we can see them.

3. Revenue generation requires a lot of knowledge and creativity.

Why are these assumptions only partially accurate? I'm glad you asked. First, while it is true that revenue is produced by sales, you now know that all employees can contribute to the company's profit. Income-generating strategies can and should come from *anyone* who has a good idea. Second, while it may be easy to look around and observe potential cost reductions, you may also see new and greater income if you look in the right places. And as for not having the needed knowledge or creativity—that's why you bought this book.

In most cases, employees are not hired to be strategists and therefore will not be asked to propose plans for the overall direction of their company. In other words: Don't hold your breath waiting for upper management to seek your opinion on a plan to grow the top-line revenue of the organization. However, each employee's actions should always be connected to company strategy. Management loves to hear from informed sources regarding new income opportunities. Therefore, you must try to understand the company's direction. Your actions can either be aligned or opposed to your company's objectives; the more aware you are of company goals, the more supportive and valuable you can be.

Figure 2.2 shows a model introduced by Igor Ansoff over 50 years ago that illustrates strategies companies can use to explore income growth options. This model has been a true workhorse since its debut and is still pertinent for you to learn how to turn your interest in company goals into an ability to enhance them. Once we review the basics, I'll modify it to illustrate where you may pull more money out of thin air for your company.

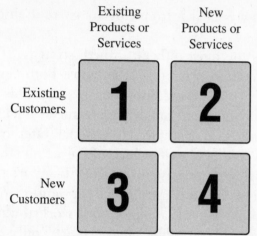

Figure 2.2   A version of the original matrix by H. Igor Ansoff, which was first published in the *Harvard Business Review*, volume 35, number 5, September/October 1957.

Area 1 represents the approach of continuing to sell existing offerings to existing customers. With this strategy, a company hopes to maximize existing customer relationships by having every customer use every offering. The strength of this growth strategy is that costs for acquiring new customers and developing new products are minimized. However, few organizations rely on this plan alone, because it does not provide for sustained, long-term growth. As an example, this is like General Motors (GM) selling more cars to their existing customers.

Area 2 demonstrates the strategy of developing new products or services not closely related to existing ones and selling them to the company's current list of customers. The company's goal with an Area 2 strategy is to take advantage of existing customer relationships, while hoping that current customers will buy new offerings. This is a product diversification strategy and is similar to GM producing personal watercraft for their current car-buying customers.

In *Area 3*, the company plans to sell its existing offerings to new customers. This is an expansion strategy. An example of this strategy is GM introducing its current automobiles in China.

Area 4 is the most difficult growth strategy. If a company intends to pursue this strategy, they must both develop a new product/service and expand into a new market. This plan is both bold and challenging and can deplete financial and human assets quickly. It is like GM trying to sell personal watercraft in China.

Can you readily identify which of these four strategies your company is using to increase income? Is it—or are they—working? If there is a clear direction, focus your efforts to achieve the goal; learn about it, talk about it, and work toward it. Bring others along with you while you're at it. You can and must do this—whether you are an executive assistant, engineer, or marketing director. To ignore it would mean disconnecting from one of the most pressing matters in your company.

If your company's declared strategy is clearly not working, you have three options. First, you could wait it out, mind your own business, do your job, and see what happens. Sadly, this lackluster approach is the one taken by most people. The second and more proactive approach is to make your best effort to find out why the strategy is not working and then propose potential solutions. Having your proposals taken seriously may depend upon your position in the company—but apply my newcomer theory. Sometimes, those new to or farthest removed from an issue have the clearest view of it. Good leaders are less concerned about the source of a solution than its quality. If a floundering strategy could be jump-started as a result of a good solution from an employee, then why couldn't that employee be you?

The third option is your opportunity to shine. If the existing strategy isn't salvageable, then the company must come up with a different, better one. That strategy could come from you as well.

Because most companies focus their growth efforts in Areas 2 and 3, they overlook the most easily reached, short-term growth available in Area 1. Many businesses have more than one product or service; yet, most of their customers fail to use all of them. What if you could encourage existing customers to use more than one company product or service? Better yet, do you see a pattern where large clusters of customers might benefit from using more of your offerings but currently are not? If so, you have a ready-made proposal for income growth of the easiest kind—selling existing products/services to existing customers. This plan is particularly good in difficult economic conditions, because it can be readily implemented, and is less expensive than any of the other three strategies. After all, there are no product development costs or substantial marketing and advertising costs; you're simply utilizing present relationships and offerings to increase sales. Granted, this strategy focuses more on swiftly generating cash as opposed to sustainable growth; but there are times when increased cash can mean the difference between life and death for a company. Propose this line of attack as an interim step toward a more sustainable-growth plan of action like that in Area 1.5.

Area 1.5? There is no Area 1.5! Well—yes, there is. It's just hidden in the model between Areas 1 and 2. Here comes the modification, as promised. I have invented the 1.5 strategy in order to show you a tremendous opportunity to add value. As seen in Figure 2.3, it's placement between Areas 1 and 2 is due to its close relationship to both.

For your company, Area 1.5 may contain more potential growth than all of the other four strategies combined. An Area 1.5 strategy is defined by a company offering products/services that customers purchase *in connection with* standard Area 1 products. At the same time, customers are more likely to buy Area 1 products because of the Area 1.5 offerings. This synergistic strategy holds more appeal for buyers than either Area 1 or 1.5 separately. You see, a 1.5 offering is not really a stand-alone product or service, because it is so closely connected to the existing offering that it could not be sold without it. A terrific

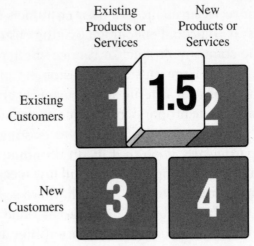

Figure 2.3

example of a 1.5 offering is GM's OnStar service, which is a GPS tracking system that can call for help after a crash, unlock the car when the keys have been locked inside, locate the car when stolen, and so forth. OnStar wouldn't be sold without the vehicle, which in turn is more appealing because of OnStar.

Such 1.5 strategies can dramatically enhance both the top line (sales revenue) and the bottom line (net profit). I recently saw a full-page ad from GM regarding OnStar in the *Wall Street Journal* that read, "Twelve years ago, General Motors created OnStar to help save lives. 100,000 crashes later, our mission remains unchanged." Since its origin, OnStar has become a huge success, bringing in high net-profit revenue and distinguishing GM's existing products from those of its competitors. That 1.5 distinction is paramount in the eyes of some GM customers. A number of buyers choose GM cars largely for the safety and security that OnStar provides. Regardless of GM's ultimate fate, OnStar has been a winning 1.5 strategy.

This example may seem a little overwhelming because of the size of the company and the cost of the product; so, let's explore a few less-intimidating examples. Last week, I took my car to my mechanic for an annual safety and emissions inspection, and he proposed a 1.5 service related to the basic service of inspecting my car. For an extra $10, the mechanic offered to send my payment and paperwork to the county tax commission and put a new registration sticker for this year on my license plate. In the past, registration has always been my hassle. I would have to fill out my own paperwork, make the payment, send everything to the county myself, wait for the county to send the license tag in the mail, and then stick it on my license plate. Ten bucks? *Well* worth the convenience! This mechanic's 1.5 offering increased his sale by over 25 percent and took him only five additional minutes to accomplish. How about the fast-food worker who asks, "Would you like fries with that order?" Or, how about the landscaping contractor who offers to draw up a detailed plan for your new yard—and only charge $250 for it—*if* you use his or her services? Additional products or services linked to existing offerings can be perfect 1.5 income growth strategies!

Could—and should—your company develop a new product or service based on an existing one? Could you be the one who develops that strategy? Of course! Doing so is not hard, as long as you're willing to conduct a little research. You must understand the customer mindset before you can identify potential 1.5 offerings. Start your strategy quest by finding the answers to these two questions:

1. What must your customers spend time or money on (or worry about) *before* buying your offering?

2. What must your customers spend time or money on (or worry about) *after* buying your offering?

You can easily answer these by honing your ability to think like your customers. Better yet, ask your customers these very questions directly. Map out the decisions they make and the thought processes they use. After you understand them, focus on their buying patterns. Are they buying products and services elsewhere that your company could provide? Are there after-market (and before-market) products and services that other companies sell that are closely related to the sale of your existing offerings? Is there any reason why your company shouldn't capture this revenue as a related part of its core sale? With some observation and study, you might discover a 1.5 strategy that opens up hidden income sources for your employer:

After numerous customers complained about their inability to get financing for the purchase of our product, I proposed an in-house financing service for qualified buyers. This new service was immediately profitable due to our interest rate, and it increased product sales by $2.6 million annually. To keep up with our increase in sales, my company purchased more raw materials from our suppliers, entitling us to supplier discounts in the amount of $64,500. Savings from discounts alone generated the same amount of profit as would have been generated by $921,428 in annual product sales.

 Profit Source 3

Refunds and Rebates—Get 'Em While They're Hot

Ready to go back to the sewer? Good. Remember when I told you that I reduced my client's future sewer expense by $1,400 per month? There's more to that story. I also secured a one-time refund for three years of past overcharges. My client was very pleased to receive a check for $50,400. While the monthly $1,400 was a future cost reduction, the $50,400 was the same as new revenue. It was money that was booked as an expense, and it was long gone. To receive that cash back via a refund was like finding brand new money. Do you know of any transaction where your company paid for something but didn't receive full value? If so, you should contact the supplier and negotiate a refund or credit.

Rebates can also yield profit. The rebate is closely related to the refund and is an interesting scheme that some companies use to induce people or businesses to buy their products. You're familiar with this approach, right? You've skeptically concluded that a rebate isn't really the "free money" that the provider would have you believe it is. Instead, the rebate amount is added to the price of the product. The seller recoups the rebate amount from you at the time of purchase and still requires you to fill out all that obnoxious paperwork before you get your money back! Your negative attitude may be justified; but there are times when a rebate really is a rebate. When carmakers get into serious inventory stack-ups, they commonly use the rebate to move product.

Have you considered rebates offered by gas and electric industries? You've probably read about rate-hike requests in your local newspaper from time to time. Natural gas and electric providers must get permission from the state regulatory agency (Public Utilities Commission or Public Service Commission) before the providers may raise rates. The negotiation reads like a script:

Gas Company: "We cannot operate profitably without another rate hike."

PUC: "Taxpayers frighten us. We will deny your request."

Gas Company: "We are herewith submitting all formal, informal, important, and irrelevant stacks of irritating and ugly financial reports proving our dire need for increased revenue. You see, we must improve our pipeline in order to increase capacity for our growing population."

PUC: "Wow. Okay, maybe we can consider the hike if you will plow a certain percentage of that money back into customer rebates for energy-saving products such as insulation, programmable thermostats, weather stripping, and the like."

Gas Company: "Hmmm. This may just work . . . "

The tragic result of this drama is that most utility consumers never hear about the rebate program. It works out well: The PUC dodges the wrath of the public by requiring a rebate from an account quickly depleted to the few who know, and the gas company gets its raise. You, however, may only reap a consolation prize of a greater expense line item and confirmed skepticism.

So, don't! Look into any and all rebate programs. Often, they may cover the entire cost of energy-efficient improvements, so they are indeed worth pursuing. In addition, the improvements themselves generally provide more than enough energy efficiency to cover the rate hike from the utility, so there is a long-term net financial advantage for your company. Contact your local gas and electric utilities or view their web sites to find out if there is an active rebate program you can take advantage of now:

Taking advantage of an electric company rebate program, I proposed the installation of 30 programmable thermostats, 47 light-switch timers, and 63 infrared occupancy sensors. The total cost of $6,250, including installation, was recouped by rebate funds. The increased energy efficiency provides annual savings of $2,500, which represents the same amount of profit earned on $35,714 in sales.

One last thought: You should also seek out federal and state rebates, grants, and incentives. Such programs range from training dollars to infrastructure creation and maintenance. They can be found by searching online and are often extremely valuable if you qualify and have the patience to wade through the paperwork. In this section, utility programs were highlighted due to their simplicity and ease of implementation.

Improve Every Process and Earn by Every Improvement

You may have heard of or participated in process improvement. If you have, you know that to improve any process is to make it more efficient by simplifying or streamlining it. Virtually any employee can identify inefficiencies if given some basic clues of what to look for. If we reduced the broad field of process improvement to just three basic concepts, we could say the following:

1. Whenever you touch something, you lose money.
2. Whenever something or someone sits and waits, you lose money.
3. Whenever something is communicated unnecessarily, you lose money.

If you can reduce how often these circumstances occur in any process, you will save money. Look around at the established ways in which your company operates—whether in production, data storage and backup, shipping, reporting, billing, or any other repeating process. You will be amazed at how many of these drags on efficiency and money you will find all around you. Keep a legal pad or voice recorder with you when you move about your workplace and perform your job, and capture any instance where you encounter inefficient processes. I'll offer red-flag clues that should alert you to such situations that you may be able to remedy.

Whenever You Touch Something, You Lose Money

- Does the company frequently move the same piles or pallets of material in order to clear work and storage space or to gain access to other areas or materials?
- Could you go digital rather than handling paperwork?
- How many steps could be saved by reducing unnecessary handoffs within your company?
- When you follow a process from start to finish, do you see anyone who doesn't need to be a part of it?
- If a product is made for your customers outside of your company, can the manufacturer drop-ship to your customer instead of your company?
- Can a decision-making process be changed to require an immediate decision rather than revisiting the same one multiple times?
- How many times do you or other employees touch the same piece of paper before someone finally deals with it? Can you reduce that number to one?
- Can anything in your company be discarded rather than stored?
- How do customers access necessary records?
- Can the process of retrieving archived analog and digital information be simplified?
- How are the component parts necessary to create finished products purchased, transported, received, stored, and moved within the facility?

- How are finished products stored, examined for quality, packaged, shipped, and invoiced?

- What is the process for calculating hourly workers' time sheets or punch cards?

- How is travel requested, approved, booked, paid for, and reimbursed? Who has to touch this process, and how long does it take?

- What does it take to get a contract out or signed? What about user manuals, warranty information, training manuals, employee handbooks, and so on?

- What is the process for customer refunds or exchanges?

- What is the process for taking a new product from the initial idea to the customer—including designing, prototyping, testing, tooling, sourcing, manufacturing, and servicing? How long does it take?

- How does your company capture and protect its intellectual property? What is the process, and how long does it take to secure a patent?

Whenever Something or Someone Sits and Waits, You Lose Money

- Do departments, teams, or individuals frequently wait for information from other departments, teams, or individuals in order to accomplish business objectives?

- Are parts regularly bottlenecking somewhere in your production line?

- Are customers constantly waiting because of production or delivery times?

- Does the entire company, department, or division stop dead in its tracks when a key employee is absent? Does the company have an understudy or cross-training process?

- If you work with overseas vendors, what is the process for accommodating disjointed time zones?

- Do language barriers interfere with the efficient transfer of information, necessitating a translator?

- Do you have more preassembly inventory than you can use in a short period of time?

- Does the company back up and archive data that only need to be saved for short-term use? Could you rotate storage media instead of buying new media every time you back up?

At my suggestion, management implemented an e-mail protocol whereby every intracompany e-mail that was critical to the success of the business (pending sales, customer needs, production deadlines, etc.) had the words "reply requested" in the subject line. This became our internal code to communicate urgency. This process change resulted in quicker turnaround times for product completion and delivery. The direct financial benefit to the company equaled $75,000 in annual net profit, which is what the company would have netted from $1,071,428 in sales revenue. This advantage continues indefinitely.

Whenever Something Is Communicated Unnecessarily, You Lose Money

- Do your colleagues follow irrelevant e-mail threads?

- Do you and your coworkers copy e-mails to unnecessary recipients simply to "cover your anatomy"?

- Are your monthly or quarterly reports useful or even read?
- Can you eliminate the unnecessary sections of your reports?
- Can your company reduce the number or length of meetings?
- Is there a better way to communicate the essential points of any meeting without physically holding it?
- Could you provide an agenda template and basic checklist of meeting management methods to be used when meetings *are* necessary?

Improved the processes for holding company meetings by eliminating unnecessary meetings and managing those that were necessary more efficiently. The financial benefit to the company amounted to $76,000 per year in personnel expenses, as well as more available time to focus on customer and operational concerns.

Perfecting the Process: Paring Down Variance and Waste

The perfect process is one that's repeated in the same exact way every time it is engaged, with no variations or waste whatsoever. Of course, there are very few perfect processes. But reducing variations and waste within any process will save time and money. So, variation (or variance) and waste are the mortal enemies of efficiency and profit.

Some businesses do not have the luxury of significantly reducing variance in their main product and service processes, because they custom tailor each offering for each client. In these instances, many processes are one-time-only occurrences that will not be repeated for other clients. This type of company is called a "job shop," because they do a different job for each customer. Naturally, their custom work is more expensive than a stock product because of variance. Cabinet work is a good example of this. Instead of purchasing stock cabinet fronts and boxes that are mass produced, customers may opt to have a cabinetmaker measure their kitchens and produce unique cabinets according to their size and style demands. Yet, even within job shops, there are still processes that should repeat with as little variance as possible.

A "production shop," on the other hand, provides the same product or service for every customer and therefore has more opportunity to eliminate variance from its core operations, since it runs in repetitive production mode. Into which of these two categories does your company fall, and where are there chances to reduce variance? If your company has multiple locations, one small move toward a standardized process can produce big rewards:

After improving my own success rate in selling point-of-purchase discount memberships, I proposed that the company standardize the changes I made to the process. Within three weeks of implementation, 2,000 cashiers working in multiple locations company wide were selling an average of one additional membership per shift. This improved company cash flow by $1.1 million per month.

Waste is the second target for elimination when improving the company's processes. It is the tag-team partner of variance that is waiting in the corner to help wrestle your company's efficiency to the mat. Every company must use its precious and finite resources wisely and efficiently. So, what are those resources? Here are some ideas:

Material

Equipment utilization

Energy

Time

Effort

Motion

Brainpower

Discretionary effort

Employee knowledge and experience

Independent judgment

Opportunity

Employee relations

Customer goodwill

"Waste" is a broader category than you might think. For example, narrowly defined, waste is the scrap material remaining from a given production process. But more broadly applied, waste is any missed opportunity, such as failing to utilize employee knowledge. As you search for wasted or unused resources, consider broader applications than others have considered, and you'll find money that others cannot see.

One example of waste reduction is engaging the knowledge and experience of the people in your company. As an example, does your company require management approval for refunds that are usually given anyway? Why not skip that step by educating customer service employees about refund policies and allowing them to handle the refund requests on their own?

While working in the customer service department, I improved the complaints process. Instead of requiring management approval for every refund or remedy, the new procedure relies upon the independent judgment of each customer service team member. One outcome has been a 34 percent improvement in customer satisfaction, loyalty, and purchase intention ratings. A direct financial benefit of $32,000 per year has resulted from less in total refunds paid and less management time expended. This amount is equivalent to the profit produced by $457,142 in company sales.

Profit
Source **5**

Catch Costly Mistakes Quickly, *Before* They Get Out the Door

My first job was at McDonald's, and it was long enough ago that the manager required all cashiers to use abacuses to calculate the math. Well, okay, that's an exaggeration—but cashiers *were* required to calculate appropriate change with their own subtraction skills. We had no computers. So, of course I made a lot of errors my first day while making change for customers. At the end of the day, my cash register was way off. At closing, the manager sat me down in his office to read me the Riot Act. I was almost fired—it was that bad. I did much better on the second day, you'll be happy to know. By day three, my accuracy was 100 percent, and I was able to sell Big Macs with confidence from that moment on—until I quit a week later.

Despite my short tenure at McDonald's, I learned an important lesson there that I still know today: Mistakes are costly, and they come in many forms. While my calculation error was simply money lost, do-overs are expensive as well. Rework will always cost more than doing the job right the first time. The indispensable employee takes great care to catch errors, regardless of their source.

Let's start with you. To err is human, and we all do it. If we learn from mistakes quickly, all is well. In an effort to learn and to minimize the chances of an error reaching a customer, examine your own performance. Have you made many mistakes in your job? Have you repeated the same slip-ups multiple times? If you need help, ask for it. Do whatever it takes to improve as soon as you can. Habitual mistakes work against your personal P&L, and they can get you fired. If, on the other hand, you are setting records for the least scrap, highest close rate per month, or most accurate engineering specifications, then you may be ready to expand your vision to include what is happening around you.

While taking care to watch for your own mistakes is important, spotting those of coworkers elevates your indispensability to that of upper management or even owner. Top people in any organization see things that less-engaged employees or customers may not, and they are very sensitive to the consequences of an incorrect, incomplete, or defective order making its way out the door of the company. While an employee may view a "small" screw-up as "just a mistake" or "no big deal," the indispensable worker recognizes the negative impact of such an error. One mistake may cost the company a potential relationship and future income. Moreover, such errors may damage the company's reputation as word of the mistake spreads amongst customers. You see, most employees who watch a customer spend $10 might think, "No big deal. If we lose that customer, we only lose $10." But savvy business people understand that this same customer may spend $350 annually and tell dozens of people who might also spend that much annually why they shouldn't do business with you. It also may have cost the company several hundred dollars in advertising costs to get that customer in the first place. It's not hard for that $10 loss to turn into a $5,000 loss. Chief executive officers know that, and you should, too.

Dealing with mistakes means being willing to acknowledge and confront them. As you do so, your interest shifts from merely looking out for yourself to carefully guarding your employer's reputation:

Having observed several costly mistakes in fulfillment due to inaccurate information, I proposed that IT audit their entire database of customers, starting with high-volume purchasers first. The effort uncovered 945 material errors, such as missing contracted restocking shipments, outdated product specs, and inaccurate contact information. After the audit and corrections, rework and reshipping cost reductions were realized in the amount of over $185,000 in the first year, which is equal to the net profit from $2,642,857 in company sales. Also, additional sales in the amount of $455,000 were directly attributable to this initiative.

If your job performance already embraces this caliber of company allegiance, wonderful! Keep it up. If, however, you are not yet there but want to be, you may have to get past a few attitudes that modern culture could have ingrained into you. Let me identify a few mistake-perpetuating attitudes, each with its more worthwhile, corresponding indispensable attitude.

It's not my job.

It's everyone's job, and if these things don't get done correctly, we might all lose our jobs.

They don't pay me enough to do that stuff.

If I never do that type of thing, I can never hope to be paid for it.

If someone else looks bad because they messed up, that only makes me look better.

If I make someone else look good, who knows—maybe they'll return the favor someday.

If I pretend I didn't see it, I can't be held responsible.

If I'm going to act more responsibly, I can't pretend I didn't see it.

Happily, upgraded and indispensable attitudes and actions are readily noticed by coworkers and supervisors. There is often a dramatic payback for employees who engage these new behaviors. Here's a case in point: One company I owned was having a hard time fielding incoming phone calls. At times, the call load was too much for our lone receptionist, and customers sometimes couldn't get through to us. This mistake was costing us customer satisfaction. To better serve customers, we requested that everyone in the office answer his or her extension whenever an incoming call rang three times. Many reacted with a modern culture attitude that answering calls wasn't their job and they weren't getting paid for it. Some never once answered that third ring. However, one employee, if not already on a call, picked up on the third ring every time he could. He was a member of the sales team, and he often found himself servicing others' customers—a task for which he was paid nothing. But his compensation eventually came. One day, he picked up on the third ring as he typically did. It was a new customer with a very large order. The commission he received on that order as well as subsequent commissions from this now-loyal customer paid him well for his indispensable willingness to step up and help the company succeed.

If Mistakes *Do* Get Out the Door, Recover Lost Customers

Sometimes there is no salvation, and a major company mistake alienates a customer who ends the relationship with great acrimony. But there are some compelling reasons why you should not write off that customer:

1. A satisfied customer tells two people, while a dissatisfied customer can tell thousands.[4]

2. A renewed customer brings a restored revenue stream to your company.

3. Reconciling with a lost customer is an excellent opportunity for you to demonstrate unusual value to your company.

4. Some former customers may be more disgruntled with their current provider than they ever were with your company. It might be easier than you think to bring them back.

First, you must consider which member of your organization should attempt to resuscitate the relationship. If you have a sales or customer service history with a former customer, your position may help you restore their loyalty. However, if you have never directly interacted with alienated customers, you may be in a position only to propose an attempt at customer renewal. Use good judgment in how you proceed with—and who you include in—this endeavor. Also, this type of work is practical only where former customers are of sufficient size to justify the time you and others will be spending on bringing them back. Again, your best judgment is important here.

How do you mend this fence without driving a nail through your thumb? Good question. Emotions are often high in these situations, as a company mistake may have caused your customer significant embarrassment and expense. The first thing to do is to gain a basic understanding of what went wrong—at least from your company's viewpoint. Next, contact the customer and set up a meeting. I suggest that the meeting be held in person, if possible. As you can imagine, this is a delicate and awkward situation. Take comfort in the reassurance that you have little to lose. The most crucial step in gaining the customer's renewed trust is to listen. While opening up a dialogue is difficult, there is no substitute for the information you will receive directly from the former customer. Never rely exclusively on what you find out about the situation from your company. Listen, ask questions, and show your understanding in order to demonstrate that you acknowledge and validate the other person's thoughts, feelings, and conclusions. Customers who have been let down will not come back unless they feel understood first. Ask every question that might allow the customer to talk until there is nothing left to say. Get everything out in the open, and express complete understanding of their position. While you may not completely agree with their conclusions, you must understand them, and the customer must feel as though you get it.

It requires a lot of discipline and skill to patiently listen as the customer relives the pain of the experience that caused the dissolution. However, your objective in this meeting is to discover what your company cost this customer. So, steel your nerves. Don't attempt to explain or justify your company's actions. Likewise, don't rush to the good news that your company has corrected the challenges that frustrated this customer. Don't try to set the record straight, even when the customer's version of the facts does not correspond with your own. Just listen and reflect back. You want the customer's side of the story now. Was the product defective? Was the order incomplete? Did you miss a critical deadline? Did the mistake cost the customer real money, and if so, how much? Your customer's expense may have assumed the form of money, embarrassment, a lost customer of his or her own, a delayed product launch, or any number of negative consequences. End the meeting with one final question to the customer: "Will you allow us to figure out a way to make up for the trouble we have caused?" Most often, the answer to this question is yes, particularly after the customer has voiced all frustrations with no defensiveness from you. Keep in mind that you are not yet asking for a renewed relationship. Frankly, any attempt to do so at this point would probably end in failure. Instead, set a tentative second meeting, pending your company's ability to propose an acceptable form of compensation for the mistake. Remain noncommittal about the exact type of compensation you might offer.

After learning the former customer's side of the story, take steps to alert your company and rectify the error. The last thing you want is to win back customers only to lose them again to the same problem; any hope of redemption would then be permanently lost. Maybe your company has already addressed the problem, but make certain of this before responding to the customer. If the problem has not yet been solved, gain the cooperation of those necessary to the solution by pointing out that if this mistake impacted this customer, it could easily happen to many more. The push for a solution is therefore based on a desire to improve the company's ability to serve many customers—not just one customer that may never do business with you again.

With a newly approachable customer and a solution in place to succeed in the future, you are ready to put together a compensation offer. Include all necessary decision makers in this phase of the effort. Your plan should be creative, have real value, and be somewhat equal to the perceived pain or cost experienced by your customer. Above all, offer the plan to your customer as part of a continuing relationship. This could be in the form of a rebate of an acceptable percentage of their total business per year, given until your company has paid an amount of money that makes up for the cost of the past bumps in the relationship. It could be a certain discount rate, again to end when a predetermined cumulative amount is reached. The longer the payment time, the longer they will remain your customer. Just make sure the rebate or discount is large enough to be enticing to them and small enough to work for your company. Be creative and generous in crafting a mutually desirable approach.

With a compensation plan in hand, you are ready to approach the customer. In this meeting, the first words out of your mouth should be, "We apologize for the past mistakes we made. We were wrong, and we caused you some real problems. Today, we are happy to have a plan to compensate you for your trouble." A sincere apology is powerful. Studies indicate that when members of the medical community such as doctors and nurses are honest about mistakes and are fully open with patients who had bad results, the risk of litigation is significantly reduced.[5] Make a sincere apology, and you'll be ready to move to the next step in patching things up.

After you apologize, set the record straight. If you are still chafing from your inability to correct your customer's misconceptions, you may do so now. If they got their facts wrong, tell them. Just be sure to follow up with, "If I had the same impression you have had all this time, I would have been feeling the same way you have been feeling about us." Next, admit to the mistakes you did make, and verify that the customer was correct in seeing your legitimate deficiencies. Then, explain any improvements made to ensure the problems will never be repeated. Finally, present the compensation offer. A good dual question to ask at this point is, "Can you accept our apology, and do you have any interest in taking advantage of our offer?" Once you ask this question, shut up. If you continue talking, you may lose the deal. Wait for the answer. Give the customer time to think and respond. You may have to tolerate an awkward silence, but the longer it is, the greater the chance of a positive outcome.

When the answer is yes, move forward, and watch that customer's orders closely. Make sure things go well. The interesting thing about a salvaged customer relationship is that it's almost always more solid after reconciliation than if there had been no problem in the first place. When things *do* go wrong—and when you can fix mistakes and get back on track—customers feel as though they've been listened to, validated, dealt with fairly, and well served. The deeper interaction required by this process always yields a stronger relationship.

When the answer is no, have a backup compensation offer ready to give your former customer. This should be something small that is not financially dependent on future customer purchases. Be cordial and grateful for the time they've given you. As you might guess, the best way to eventually get back the ex-customer who at first rejects a reconciliation offer is to graciously accept the negative answer, give something of nominal value that is not expected, and check back at some point in the near future to see how the gift worked out for their business. Another dialogue may be possible at that time:

Revived a customer relationship that was dormant for two years due to mistakes on our part. While the customer was at first reluctant to work with us again, I offered a custom-tailored incentive package and won the business back. During the next year, this customer's purchases amounted to $275,000.

Print Money at Work by Doing Your Own Job Better

7 Profit Source

If you're feeling daunted by the idea of creating proposals to increase profits and of seeking others' approval, then this section is for you. You can contribute financially to your company simply by regulating yourself. By improving your own job performance—that is, the quantity or quality of your work—you add value to your company.

Stay on Task

> Time management is desirable, but disruption management is critical.

To improve the amount of work you produce, you need to spend more time doing job-related tasks and less time doing everything else. In a 2005 survey, the average employee admitted to wasting 2.09 hours per eight-hour workday.[6] In a similar 2007 survey, employees admitted wasting an average of 1.7 hours per eight-hour workday.[7] If you really evaluate where your time goes, you will be shocked to discover how much of your paid working time is wasted. Time management is important, and there are countless methods, systems, and tools to help you establish priorities and keep you focused on the highest-value tasks first. Choose a system and use it religiously.

Disruption Management = Self Discipline + Interpersonal Skills

When you begin to manage your time more efficiently, the challenge of minimizing interruptions by others often becomes more critical than arranging time to accomplish your tasks. In the course of an average day, you are interrupted and sidetracked by coworkers, managers, e-mails, IMs, text messages, meetings, landline calls, and cell phone calls. You have to minimize these productivity robbers and stay focused on your primary work. Stop enabling and getting sucked into the inefficiencies of others—however pressing or engaging those issues may appear to be. Your first response to someone who may perhaps inadvertently drain your time should be, "I'm on a deadline." Learn to use that phrase early and often. If possible, stick a note on your closed door alerting the world to your deadline and requesting that your door remain shut unless there is a fire in the building. A note at the entrance to a cubicle will accomplish the same thing. Unless you have an open-door management policy, consider getting rid of those extra chairs near your desk. They invite interlopers to plop down and crash your efficiency. After being rebuffed a few times, those who have no justifiable reason for disrupting your work will get the idea. Be considerate of others' feelings, of course, and treat them with respect, but get out of these interactions before wasting too much time.

You may achieve disruption management not only by improving your interpersonal skills but by enhancing your self-discipline as well. When necessary, consider turning off your cell phone and only checking voice messages once or twice a day. I wouldn't make this recommendation if I hadn't written this book.

In order to corner and preserve enough quiet time to write, it was necessary to turn off my cell phone. Eliminating that persistent distraction has tremendously increased my productivity and convinced me to turn it off as needed in order to accomplish other time-sensitive tasks in the future. I still communicate with the world but on a schedule of my choosing. While a wonderful productivity tool, e-mail is too frequently just another medium for disruptions and should be handled similarly. Check and respond to messages at a regular time once or twice a day. I generally deal with e-mails first thing in the morning and again in the early afternoon.

Another insidious self-imposed distraction is the Internet. Studies show that the average worker spends six to eight hours per week in non-job-related surfing.[8] Be disciplined in your cyber behaviors, and you'll free up a whopping 350 hours per year for your real job.

Some of these methods for improving your productivity will work for you, and some will not—depending on your position, company, and workplace policies. Be creative and do all you can to remain focused on the core activities that make up your job. Managing time and disruptions requires self-discipline and a moderate level of interpersonal skill. If you are serious about increasing your personal output and financial contribution to your company, you have no choice but to take charge of your time and attention.

Manage Quality

> *The perfect is the enemy of the good.*
> —Voltaire

In order to contribute financially by improving your performance, you must also dispassionately evaluate the quality of your work. Some people do shoddy work and need to drastically improve quality, while many others take pride in producing high-quality work. There is another category of workers who—perhaps surprisingly—thwart efficient output by pursuing perfection when it is not necessary. Many times, something short of perfection is good enough. The amount of resources used to achieve perfection is enormous compared to what is needed to yield a product or service that will surprise and delight a customer.

If you fall outside the spectrum of the obsessive-compulsive worker but still want to do a great job, how do you gauge the amount of effort necessary to achieve greatness? What are your quality targets, and where are you performing in relation to them? If you don't know your expected level of quality or how close you are to hitting it, find out now. Your direct manager is your best source for these answers. Asking about such targets will please both your manager and your customers. Discuss overall company standards as well as those related to the performance for your particular job so that there is no misunderstanding. The scale found in Figure 2.4 may guide your discussion.

I recommend that you consistently produce a little higher quality than is required of you. Take pride in doing your job better than is expected by going beyond your assigned quality goal—but not by *too* much. To paraphrase Voltaire, perfection is the enemy of the good, because it goes too far beyond the target to be worth the extra time, money, and energy; often, that

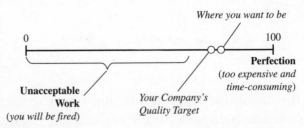

Figure 2.4

last little bit of quality is not even noticeable to customers. But improving the quality of your work is an energizing practice that will add value to your company and interest to your activities.

Use Your Brain

> Brain utilization in humans is typically around 10 percent until they go to work, at which time it quickly drops to 5 percent.

Engaging your gray matter will dramatically increase the quality and quantity of your work. Because most jobs are repetitive (or have portions that are), it is easy to operate on autopilot. Working without thinking is an all-too-common problem, which, if left uncorrected, will impede your ability to add value to your company and progress in your career. Virtually every profit-enhancing idea found herein requires you to commit more brain power to company issues than you may have used before. These suggestions simply cannot be accomplished without some serious thought. While we've discussed much of the planning component to change, cerebral bandwidth is also crucial. I am convinced that thinking ability improves with exercise. Challenge yourself to step up and become more interesting, useful, and intellectually potent. There are four distinct sources you should explore in order to upgrade your mental database and abilities to the end that you can perform better on the job. Let's look at them now.

Formal Education
What is your current education level? What will it take to reach the next level? Rightly or wrongly, your current manager—as well as future employers—will tie your value in the company to the amount of formal education you have obtained. Accordingly,

if you don't have a high school diploma or GED, get it now. If you have graduated from high school but have not graduated from a college or university, you should start the process of getting a bachelor's degree now. If you have a bachelor's degree, you may want to seriously consider a graduate program that could fit into your work and family schedule. Because companies benefit directly from a more educated workforce, they often pay part or all of the costs. Check with your employer and make plans to increase your formal education.

Aside from enhancing your resume, higher education will provide you with knowledge and skills that will directly contribute to your job performance. If your company bills your hours directly to clients at a certain rate, your formal education could move you to a higher billing rate. If this is the case, furthering your education is an obvious way to add value to your company and increase your income at the same time. Are you worried about how long it will take to advance your education? So what if it takes four years to get a degree? Those four years will pass, whether you're in school or not. You may as well make them productive and profit enhancing.

Informal Education

Your second-grade teacher was right: Reading *is* good. Every time you open a nonfiction book, you expose your mind to a highly focused and organized set of facts, methods, and experiences that increase your knowledge and abilities in that field. Nonfiction is a fantastic source of practical information on every subject imaginable because of what I call the "law of concentration." To write a nonfiction book, an author must draw together all the passion, mistakes, successes, research, techniques, shortcuts, and history of a personal journey of learning, that has taken years—if not a lifetime—to accumulate. This exercise in concentration involves weeding out the unnecessary and superfluous so that only the most useful portions of a much larger body of information make it onto the pages of the finished product. While some books are clearly better than others, there is always at least one nugget of information—and more often, many of them—that you can use to change your life for the better.

I am a big fan of nonfiction books and own over 400 of them on the subject of business alone. Reading each one has allowed me to gain insights that have helped with relevant business issues. They then become references when specific questions arise, as is often the case. Books or industry journals related to your business might be especially useful for you in adding value to your company. Develop an appetite for knowledge and satisfy that hunger by devouring the rich, concentrated writings of nonfiction authors.

World and Economic Events

How plugged in are you to what is happening in global, national, and local settings? Things are constantly changing on all fronts, and staying informed is more imperative now than ever before. Newspapers, the Internet, news magazines, and daily newscasts are essential sources of information that will add relevance to your job. I recommend that you subscribe to the *Wall Street Journal* to get a daily update of global and national business, market, and political developments. Reading the *Wall Street Journal* will quickly increase your financial vocabulary and understanding.

Next, you should attempt to get up to speed on what is happening locally, perhaps through your town or village newspaper. It is amazing how often a story from the morning news will serve you later in your workday. Many decisions you make can be more informed by a regular dose of information that, surprisingly, many of your coworkers don't access. Information is an advantage to you as you continue to differentiate yourself from the average employee in your company. The old saying is true: Information *is* power.

Customer Needs

The importance of knowing customer needs and how and when they change over time cannot be overstated. When a company fails, it's often due to a lack of knowledge about what its customers have wanted and needed along the way. If your company does not respond to changing customer demands faster and more accurately than the competition, then it, too, runs the risk of becoming endangered or extinct.

What can you do to keep your organization competitive? The main thing is to listen to your customers. Hearing customer demands is most easily (and most traditionally) accomplished by sales, marketing, and customer service teams. In more innovative and responsive firms, CEOs and upper-management teams will lend an ear as well. My personal belief is that the companies that will thrive in the next five years are those that learn about customer preferences through employees at all levels and all positions. Corporate financial success cannot hinge merely on traditional and formal customer contacts and measures that utilize only a handful of players. The effort must be much broader. You can participate in this information-gathering effort by asking customers how well your company is serving them each time you contact them. Ask if they have any ideas about how you can better meet their needs. Ask if there is any company in the market that is doing a better job of providing what they want. My favorite customer question comes from my former partner Mike Carter: "On a scale of 1 to 10, how are we doing—and how can we get to a 10?"

If you don't have any occasion for direct contact with customers in your job, there are still measures you can take to remain sensitive to customer demand. You can at least notice when demand for a product or service is diminishing or increasing, or you can talk to friends about how your company is perceived in the market. You might run into customers in more casual settings such as civic groups, community or cultural events, and other social gatherings. Try to get a sense of how they perceive your company and what the competition is presenting to them. Management needs to be aware of such information and any possible improvement it may prescribe for the company. If the number of company members sensitive to customer perception and demand is multiplied considerably, the longevity of your company and job may be preserved.

Tuned In, by Craig Stull, Phil Myers and David Meerman Scott, is an excellent book on listening to customers. If you're serious about responding better to customer needs, I highly recommend it to you.

Notice how each of these four sources of information and mental power are valuable on their own. Now, imagine what could happen in your career if you engaged all of them at the same time. If you are taking advantage of none or only some of these sources of cranial power, start incorporating more of them, and observe how much more value you bring to your job, company, customers, and yourself. Who knows? Maybe you'll even begin utilizing a whopping 12 percent of your brain while at work.

Move Faster

If you do nothing else, you can actually increase your personal productivity just by picking up your pace. I'm not talking about being frantic but simply about moving a little faster. Anyone can walk more briskly, keyboard more rapidly, speak a few more words per minute, read a little speedier, and perform repetitive tasks more quickly. You already do this on occasion. Think about those times when you have a deadline for a report or presentation. What about the last day before that extended vacation? The most productive day of my life was the day before a two-week trip to Switzerland. I still have the to-do list with all 32 items checked off, each a major task. The list reminds me of how productive I can be just by speeding up. A sense of urgency always helps you get more done. Speed up, and your workday will go by in the blink of an eye. Quicken your pace, and your reputation for being essential to the company will grow.

Get Creative

Whether you are trying to perform your own job in better ways or searching for profit enhancing ideas, the more creative you can be, the more indispensable you will become. However, creativity is such a huge topic area, it is a book unto itself. I recommend *A Whack on the Side of the Head* by Roger von Oech.

Profit
Source **8**

How I Spent My Summer Vacation—Finding $500,000 in New Zealand

I was consulting for a global oil company in Sydney, Australia one summer (summer for me—winter in that hemisphere) when I was given some great instruction by my former partner and rabid fisherman Al Switzler. He advised, "If you're going to be in that part of the world, you absolutely must stop in New Zealand and fish the Tongariro River." Without hesitation, I tacked on a three-day fishing excursion to the back-end of the consulting trip. The consulting work in Sydney was, by itself, quite successful; however, the real achievement was in New Zealand, where I truly landed a fish "this big."

The Tongariro is New Zealand's most-fished river. It is also one of the best trout rivers in the world. For much of the year, the trout—75 percent rainbows and 25 percent browns—live in nearby Lake Taupo, where they eat well and grow increasingly larger. During the winter months, they run upriver to spawn and take their dinner-table chances. The flow of the river is fairly strong, and when a fish gets hooked, it will run extremely fast and hard, either up- or downstream. The combination of fish size, strength, and direction of run makes for some of the most exciting trout fishing one could ever experience.

When I fished the river, the first trout on my line was not a disappointment. Just as it took the fly, I yanked hard to set the hook, and my future food immediately began its escape attempt by speeding upstream against the current. It was shocking how fast the line spun out. It released a high and otherworldly pitch as the reel spat out much of its length. Before the reel had disgorged its full contents, the trout tired, slowed, and reversed direction. The flow of the river had served as my ally, exhausting my prey as it tried to outrun me. Semi-spent, the hapless fish was carried back downstream, where I netted it fairly easily. I repeated my fishing conquest a few times as my guide and I secured several meals. Foolishly, I felt my novice experience had tamed the Tongariro. After all, I had collected some colorful fish stories, taken some stunning photographs, and garnered serious bragging rights for my next conversation with my partner.

And then I hooked a Monster of the Tongariro.

Unlike the victims on the riverbank, this creature ran the more intelligent and fish friendly direction of downstream. For others out there who partake in this hobby: Have you ever been fishing and thought, "Gee, I wonder how much line is in my reel?" I have. I thought about that when the reel started squealing and created a 45-mile-per-hour wind in my face as it quickly began to empty, and suddenly I knew I wouldn't have enough line. In fact, no reel could have held enough, and no line would have been strong enough to avert the inevitable. All I could do was watch helplessly as the spool of fishing line disappeared at an astounding pace beneath the security of the Tongariro's crests.

Finally, when the last, small chance of salvaging this situation came about; when that frail knot at the end of the coil would have its big moment; just when I would be able to tell the most fantastic story of how, at the last inch of line, I caught the biggest rainbow trout in this entire river—*tink*.

When that line broke, so did my heart. To this day, I wonder if towing a whole spool of fishing line from its mouth has made that trout less attractive to potential spawning partners. I take comfort in the probability that Mr. Hooklineandsinker never passed along his genes. Take that, you monster!

From Fish Story to Revenue Story

That night—while enjoying expertly prepared trout in the dining room of the wonderful Tongariro Lodge—I met a group of people having a company party. We talked for some time about New Zealand, America, politics, the world economy, and my record- and line-breaking now socially outcast fish that got away— all the normal pleasantries. We made a genuine connection, and it was a delightful and enlightening conversation.

When jet lag kicked in, I excused myself, thanked them for the enjoyable evening, and walked toward the door. Realizing that during our lengthy conversation, I never asked the simple question regarding what their business was, I turned back and asked with one foot literally outside the door, "Oh, by the way, what type of work do you do?" to which one of them responded, "We're in organizational development and consulting, mate; how about you?" This got my attention, as it was my industry as well, and we began an entirely new discussion specific to our mutual business interests and experiences.

As we talked, I learned that their company—which was head-quartered in Australia—was looking for fresh training and con-sulting content about communication, conflict resolution, team building, customer service, organizational change, efficiency, and survey services to present to their clients. My company had already created all of those offerings, and *we* were interested in finding representation for them in Australia and New Zealand. A few days after that trout dinner, I called their headquarters in Australia to confirm the match between their clients' needs and our materials. The president in Sydney immediately wanted to pursue a relationship. That question, match, and subsequent meetings brought $500,000 in licensing fees to our firm.

While on vacation, met a group of consultants who expressed a desire to use our intellectual property in their local markets. Shortly after that first meeting, negotiated a licensing fee of $500,000 USD—all net profit—for my firm. This was the amount of profit gained from $2.5 million in ordinary sales.

Income Lessons Learned

A chance or casual encounter like this is a potent opportunity to match your company's offerings with a potential customer's needs. Most people that we try to convince of an idea—or to whom we attempt to sell something—will tend to run away (and often downstream—*tink*). This is called sales resistance, and it's hardwired into everyone. It's probably a good thing, because without it, we would all be spending copious amounts of money on late-night infomercial products. As opposed to a sales contact, the chance or casual encounter is an easier entry point to a potential business relationship, because there is little or no sales resistance. After I met my new friends at the lodge and we eventually talked business, what do you suppose they reported to headquarters? Probably something along the lines of "just happened to meet a Yank who was fishing in New Zealand, who just happens to have what we need to be more useful to our clients." No resistance. Often in this scenario, prospects feel that the coming transaction is partially, if not completely, their idea. And they're right.

Take advantage of chance meetings and casual settings to match up potential customers with appropriate offerings from your company. Mingle with would-be buyers in as many informal settings as possible. And while you're there, ask a lot of questions. Determine what their most urgent needs or problems are. Figure out what areas of their business most need added value. Assess their company goals. Do all of this with the genuine objective of solving their problems and meeting their business needs. Be careful not to squander the tee time or relaxed lunch by rushing to close prospects until you know what is really important to them and what they may want to buy from you. If you are not in sales, you have an added advantage over salespeople: experiencing less sales resistance than that which they may regularly encounter. Regardless of your position, put those who are interested in your business together with the right people in your company, and do so with the promise that you will personally watch out for them from the inside as they interact with your organization.

Of course, you cannot always rely upon this kind of chance encounter. So, the next best thing is enticing prospects to contact you as a result of marketing, advertising, word of mouth, and social networking on the internet. People who respond to formal or informal marketing tend to have low or moderate sales resistance. They are contacting you and obviously have some interest in your offering. But their resistance does exist, and if they feel sales pressure, they will withdraw.

Everyone within the organization who interacts with customers—whether he or she is the CEO, a sales professional, or a customer service representative—must be prepared for the moment a customer approaches with an interest in establishing a relationship with the company. When I was president and co-owner of an organizational development consulting firm a few years ago, we received such a call. Our receptionist buzzed me over the intercom, alerting me that a woman on line three wanted to talk with the president about working with our company and would not talk to anyone in sales. Without knowing anything about this woman—except her stated opposition to sales—I picked up line three and greeted her. She told me her name and company and explained how our brochure had fallen into her hands and how she and her team had read it with some interest. Her company, a major defense contractor, was interested in making a wide-scale culture change, as they were preparing to bid on the largest contract in their company's history. She was in charge of selecting a consulting firm to procure this change and enhance their chance of winning that very important contract. Making no bones about the importance of our call, she informed me that depending on what happened in the next 30 minutes, she would either discontinue consideration of our firm or be on a plane the next day to visit us and begin talking about the project. This was someone who had preliminarily decided to use our services in a rather large way, as long as this phone call went well. I must admit that my palms started sweating just a little.

As we talked, it became apparent how delightful and professional this woman was and how thoroughly she had researched her options. I asked what her team found interesting about our company, and she had many questions of her own. We determined that this was a good match, and 30 minutes into the conversation, her visit to our firm was scheduled for the next day.

The happy ending to this story is that approximately two years later—after a multi-million dollar consulting engagement—her company did indeed win the $200 billion contract, and they were gracious enough to acknowledge our contribution to their success. One of the biggest business successes in my career—and certainly the largest client accomplishment I have ever been a part of—began with a simple phone call, where pushing too hard on my part would have killed the deal.

You can keep sales resistance at bay when a prospect approaches you by confirming *why* this person approached you in the first place. Ask and answer questions, but do not try to hurdle toward a business commitment just yet. More often than not, an interested and self-motivated prospect has preliminarily decided to buy but must first be sure there is *no* reason *not* to buy. Let the prospect satisfy himself or herself on this point, and then move to creating a contract. Your marketing department should find ways to generate prospect responses from your media advertising. Viral marketing and word-of-mouth advertising are the best stimuli, because sales resistance is lower than with traditional practices. Use any method that works to get prospects to call, e-mail, or walk in on their own.

Supply Your Suppliers with Profit—Let Them Supply Discounts in Return

One way to get discounts from suppliers is to demand them. Although this strong–arming tactic has worked for very large companies that can throw their weight around, it may produce resentment and questionable quality. A better way to get discounts is to simply ask for them; you might be pleasantly surprised. I have seen businesses receive discounts many times just by asking, and the question that seems to work well is, "Is that the best you can do?" This indispensable method is certainly something your company can try as soon as Monday. But the surest way to get the deepest supplier discounts is to help them find the money in their own organizations to offset those discounts.

After you have successfully implemented profit-increasing proposals in your company, you will find that many of them can be applied to suppliers. To get the ball rolling, ask your supplier, "Would you be willing to give us a discount on future purchases if we can show you how to recoup that money through the same profit enhancements we have used in our own company?" Simply using your proven profit initiatives will allow you to become a consultant to your suppliers. Once you have already gained an initial financial benefit by implementing indispensable initiatives, you can multiply the benefits to your company again and again. You have a group of willing participants in your supplier base. They want to maintain their relationship with you, *as long as* it's profitable for them. You're offering them a zero-cost method of strengthening the relationship and increasing the chances that you will continue to buy from them. You should agree to refrain from charging a consulting fee, provided they give an ongoing discount in pricing that matches the benefit you provide them. Watch what happens when a good idea is multiplied by a number of suppliers:

Taking advantage of an electric company rebate program, I proposed the installation of 30 programmable thermostats, 47 light-switch timers, and 63 infrared occupancy sensors. The total cost of $6,250, including installation, was covered by rebate funds, and the increased energy efficiency provides annual savings of $2,500—the same amount of profit the company realizes from $35,714 in full-margin sales. This profit contribution will repeat annually.

(continued)

(continued)

I then took this innovation to seven of our material suppliers and service providers who had not taken advantage of the rebate program. They agreed to provide our company with discounts on future purchases equal to the amount of savings they would realize from the rebates. The total of all discount amounts was $11,750 in annual net profit to our company, which was equal to the profit gained from $167,857 in sales. This profit contribution will repeat annually.

Become Indispensable to Customers by Giving *Them* Money

While you can be assertive with suppliers in establishing terms of a business relationship, you must be more circumspect with customers. Plan to share with them proven profit-building strategies, but do so with no strings attached. You may not seek the same financial incentive as you might with suppliers. Rather, offer to help in exchange for the strength of your ongoing relationship. It is important that you seek nothing in return for this benefit other than a stronger customer connection. Your goal is to make your company indispensable to your customer, and handing over methods for increasing profit is a big step in the right direction.

As you consider adding value to your customer, don't give all of your profit-enhancing secrets away at one time. Value-added customer contact is a rare and helpful practice. By getting in touch with your company's customers on a quarterly or monthly basis—and teaching yet another way for them to increase profits each time—you cement that relationship by increments. Your progressive contributions will inevitably lead to more business and longer-term relationships. It will also demonstrate to your clients that your value far surpasses that of the competition.

Teaching methods of profit enhancement is a terrific way to attract new customers and to serve existing ones. Imagine a salesperson saying to a prospective customer, "Before you make the decision to order our product, I'd like to show you how you can generate new money with which to pay for it." It isn't often that salespeople can help customers produce the funds necessary to buy their product:

In a competitive bid situation, I offered four unrelated profit-enhancing measures that were well suited to the prospect's specific business. The total estimated financial benefit of these initiatives was approximately 65 percent of our bid amount. While our actual bid was higher than any of the competitors, our team won the contract due to the unusual benefit provided by the unrelated profit enhancements. The customer reported that the net cost of our bid was the lowest when factoring in the unexpected sources of profit we provided.

Improve Company Cash Flow and Become a Hero

Do you know anyone who does not care whether they are paid their full salary after performing all of their work? Would *you* be willing to write off 100 percent of your next paycheck? Probably not! Yet, far too many organizations tend to behave as if they don't care whether they get paid for their goods and services. This problem comes about because the work or sale was not invoiced, because it was improperly or only partially invoiced, or because it was invoiced but not collected.

Let's first look at the failure to invoice. This is a bigger problem than you might imagine, because if it's time to invoice the customer, your company has already spent 93 percent of that invoice amount in fulfilling the order (assuming a 7 percent net-profit margin). At that rate, it would require the net profit from almost 14 jobs/orders of the same size to pay back the lost dollars associated with a missed invoice from just one job/order. If the company fails to bill for even a small percentage of its performed work, the firm could be in danger of going out of business. The worst part of this scenario is that management might not even know about this problem until it's too late.

If your organization's billing records haven't been audited in a long time, you might want to propose doing so now. Or, perhaps you are already aware of an instance in which your company has performed work but has not billed properly. Many employees don't concern themselves with such invoicing issues; that's exactly why *you* need to. Few behaviors mean more to an employer than that of safeguarding the cash flow of the company. It is a good idea for you to familiarize yourself with how customers are charged for your company's products and services and look for situations where money may be slipping through the cracks. Some organizations have bulletproof systems, but many do not. Even if every job/order was invoiced, are those invoices accurate? Was the correct price applied? Did we include all of the hours, extras, and add-ons? Did we give away something for free that we could have legitimately charged for? Any financial gains that come from your efforts to locate missed revenue can legitimately be referenced in your resume. My relative's updated resume reflects his important contribution:

> *Developed an innovative process for accurately capturing legitimate billing opportunities that were being missed by the company. During the first year of implementation, the process resulted in invoicing over $150,000 in additional revenue that otherwise would have been lost. This bottom-line contribution is equal to the profit earned by the company on a $5 million contract.*

Okay, so the customer has received the product or service and has been correctly billed. Now what? Well, they need to pay up. In some industries—like airline, hotel, retail, and others—the customer pays the bill before or at the time the product or service is received. When money is paid up front, no collection problem exists unless the buyer disputes the credit card bill or writes a bad check. Obviously, companies that collect money up front have good cash flow.

In many other industries, however, the money isn't collected until 10, 30, 60, or even 90 days or more after the product or service is delivered. If your company falls into the delayed-collection category, there are some improvements you can propose that can help cash flow. A simple method to improve cash flow is to match payable timing to receivables. As an example, if you get paid by customers for products and services in 30 days or less, then you should pay vendors and suppliers in 30 days or more.

However, timing alone won't relieve cash flow concerns if a large percentage of the company's financial obligation is payroll. Pushing that significant cost out an extra 30 days is rarely feasible. Such was the situation for one of my recent clients. His service company was suffering from tremendous cash flow challenges due to the nature of his business model. This company had a lengthy cycle for converting services into cash payments from customers. First, they had to meet payroll and other expenses, then provide services to customers, then invoice customers, and then wait 30 to 60 days for customer payment. A model of the Cash Conversion Cycle (CCC) for my client's business revealed that his company spent money at the beginning of the cycle in order to fulfill customer contracts 75 days before the customers paid invoices for that same work (see Figure 2.5).

It was no longer possible for my client to finance his customers in this way. Something had to change, drastically and immediately, or his company's extinction loomed in his near future. So, I recommended that he reduce the number of days in the company's CCC. In short, he absolutely *had* to begin billing and collecting in advance for the company's services. Eventually, all of the company's customers agreed to start paying in advance, and all remained loyal customers. After the first month and initial

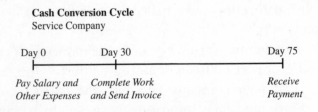

Figure 2.5

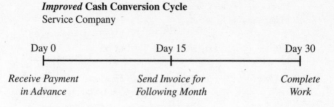

Figure 2.6

pain of the policy change, the customers were on virtually the same monthly payment timetable as they had been before. Their inconvenience was minimal. However, the billing cycle change was the difference between flourishing and extinction for my client. The previous cash flow problems were instantly solved. The new CCC model for that business is surprisingly different from the old one (see Figure 2.6).

As you can see, the timing for the CCC is zero days. The company no longer carries its customers, has no need of credit lines, and can ride out whatever financial storm the economy might bring. Moreover, because they don't use credit to meet their obligations, interest charges are a distant memory. The business is now more profitable than ever before—and has managed to become so without raising prices. Even better, new customers accept the payment policy with no complaints. In the future, my client can grow the business as fast as an improving market will allow, without the cash flow problems that often come with growth. Had there been substantial customer resistance to the policy, I would have recommended that only a portion of the money be paid in advance—perhaps 50 percent. Can your company make such a shift in its billing policy to alleviate cash flow challenges?

If your organization manufactures a product, the CCC is a little different, and the opportunity to reduce the cycle time is even expanded.

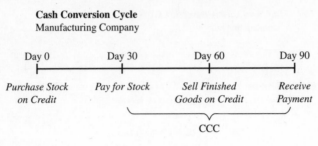

Figure 2.7

As illustrated in Figure 2.7, manufacturing companies need to purchase materials, or stock, before they can sell their product and receive their payment. The need for supplies requires the company to either pay cash for the supplies or purchase them on credit. As you can see, buying on credit can shorten the CCC, because a company can delay payment to its suppliers and thereby lessen the number of days between its cash outlay and receipt of payment from its customers. In fact, the more time a company can negotiate with suppliers before actually paying for stock ordered on credit, the fewer days in its CCC. Negotiating for payment of stock is obviously not an option for service companies, because their "stock" is personnel, and payroll cannot reasonably be delayed. Aside from the difference in timing for paying suppliers, manufacturing and service companies face the same CCC concerns. To resolve those concerns, any company should collect as much cash when the order is placed as the market will bear—up to the entire amount, if possible. Failing that, make the entire amount due upon delivery, with no credit extended.

So, if a company can reduce their CCC to very few or even zero days, life is good and cash is flowing. Can it get even better than zero days? Is that even *possible*? Will customers pay for goods and services *before* they receive them? Believe it or not, some businesses reach a negative number of days in their CCC.

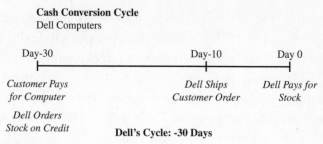

Figure 2.8

Such a cycle occurs when customers pay in advance, and the company pays for stock after receiving it to fill the order. Dell Computers may be king of the Cash Conversion Cycle. Historically, Dell has sustained a CCC of negative 40 days. In other words, it has collected cash from customers 40 days before paying suppliers. Recently, however, Dell's CCC has been tracking at around negative 30 days—not as good as its history but still impressive and undeniably helpful for cash flow (see Figure 2.8).[9]

When a company can achieve a negative CCC, it actually creates its own working capital rather than seeking credit to do so. In a tight credit market, every company should be working on reducing its CCC to the smallest number of days possible—even to a negative number of days if it can. Liquidity—or cash on hand—will always diminish if the CCC gets longer, as the company will eat cash in normal operations (because it has already paid its suppliers and is waiting for payment from customers), and it will always inhale cash during growth (because it has paid even more money to its suppliers and is waiting for even more payment from clients). You may remember my previous statement about liquidity: When a company runs out of cash—game over.

So, what does this mean for you? Plainly stated, you should look for ways to shorten your company's Cash Conversion Cycle. To assist in any way with this outcome is to contribute to the bottom line. If you're thinking that this accounting stuff is way out your realm—think again. Most people will feel the same, because unless you have an accounting background, it can seem daunting. However, you don't need to know everything about your company's CCC to change it for the better. The following are some specific changes you can propose to your employer, each of which will serve to shorten the CCC.

Shorten the accounts receivable period:

- Run receivables reports more frequently (weekly or even daily).
- Review receivables regularly in management meetings.
- Shorten the net due date on invoices.
- Stiffen—and enforce—penalties for late payments.
- Increase staff time and attention on collections.

Shorten the time inventory is sitting around at or in transit to/from your company:

- Find ways to have stock delivered faster without increasing shipping costs.
- Improve production efficiencies.
- Reduce waiting-stock inventory levels ("just-in-time" management).
- Ship finished goods immediately after completion.

Lengthen the time your company takes to pay its payables:

- Establish longer payment terms with suppliers.
- Make installment payments to stretch the average payment time.

- Don't trigger finance charges or late fees.
- Maintain goodwill with suppliers.

These three areas, in concert with each other, directly affect your company's Cash Conversion Cycle. Achieving any one of these goals will shorten the CCC, but making progress in two or all three will make a dramatic difference in the financial health of your company. For some businesses, such innovations will mean the difference between surviving and turning off the lights.

This is a huge problem (and opportunity). It is estimated that more than $950 billion is tied up in balance sheets of American companies.[10] Do whatever it takes to liberate locked-up money for use by your company by speeding accounts receivable, constraining accounts payable, and reducing inventory.

Still not confident enough to move ahead? You can also bring in a consultant to walk your company through these critical improvements. There are many competent firms that can do the up-front analysis work and even implement the new processes. Be sure to impress upon other employees the importance of these changes. If the people in your company are not engaged and enthusiastically on board, you will experience costly setbacks and delays:

After observing that our company was constantly sitting on excess inventory, I proposed a plan that reduced stock levels by 30 percent. This improvement freed up needed cash for other operations, reducing the company's need for outside credit.

Give Your Company an Unexpected Competitive Advantage

Simply stated, a company's value proposition is nothing more than a proposal to sell products and services at a given price to its customers. You say to your customers, "Pay this price for this item—it's worth it." If customers agree, it's a done deal. Your company's current value proposition is represented by the center box in Figure 2.9, but there are other options you can explore to enhance your market position in response to an ever-changing business environment. There are eight total, to be exact—each one embodying a distinctly different approach to satisfying customer desire.

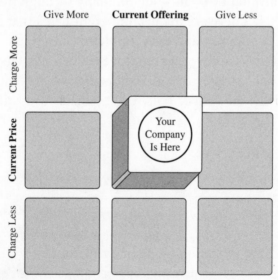

Figure 2.9

If you'd like to think inside the boxes and make them work for you, question whether your company should continue with its present value proposition or if perhaps there is a better one. The answer depends upon what customers are willing and able to pay for the products/services your organization is offering. It also depends upon your company's needs and goals. If customers are buying a company's offerings at the asking prices—and the company is making a profit—then the value proposition is, obviously, a good one. That value proposition should work well until one or more key factors change—and keep in mind that they always do. Material costs increase; the competition makes a better offer; your company's technologies or processes become obsolete; your product or industry matures; the economy implodes—any number of things can and *will* vary. Nothing remains constant. So, staying with the same strategy forever is, in a word, impossible.

If change is forcing your company to alter its current value proposition, then to where within the model should and can it move? The hard part about business strategy is matching the desires of customers with the needs and goals of the company. But this pairing is easier if you can envision the map of other price/offering options. If you understand this map, you might propose necessary changes yourself. You will at least know why your employer must at times make certain changes in strategy and be better able to support those changes. Either way, increasing your working knowledge of basic market positioning is another way you can add tremendous and unexpected value.

Market Position 1: Offer More and Raise the Price

If you perceive that customers need more from your company—and that they would be willing to pay more for it—then position 1 might be a profitable strategy for you. Try to maximize the revenue from new features, products, or services while holding your company's additional fulfillment costs to a minimum.

Obviously, if it costs more for your company to increase the offering's value than you can bring in by increasing the sales price, you should not pursue this strategy. However, companies can frequently add a tremendous amount of perceived value—which translates into a higher sales price—without a substantial increase in its production costs.

I have always been impressed with Swiss watchmakers, who seem to have no shame when it comes to pricing their high-end, solid gold watches. It is interesting that a given model of a watch with a solid gold case can cost $10,000 or $20,000 more than its stainless sibling, even though the crystal, movement, backing, band, and face are exactly the same. What is the additional manufacturing cost of the gold version? About $1,200! While the customer is receiving more value with the gold version over the stainless one, the watchmaker is reaping the larger benefit. Your company's return on investment may not be as high as the Swiss, but you get the idea. It's all about perception when it comes to customer value. What additional customer value might you propose that can be achieved by your employer at a reasonable cost? See Figure 2.10.

Market Position 2: Keep the Offering the Same and Raise the Price

At first, this approach might not seem very appealing to buyers. Why would customers be willing to pay increased prices and get nothing extra in return? It's a fair question. Years ago, when my partners and I needed to spend more time with our young families, we decided to raise our training and consulting fees. Our thinking was that some clients would pay the increased fees and some wouldn't, resulting in fewer overall days on the road. We figured we would be paid more per day while working fewer days. With some anxiety, we more than doubled our fee structure, and our offerings remained the same. To our surprise, we immediately began booking *more* days in the field—not fewer.

Figure 2.10

The More or Less Value Model, © 2010 by More or Less, Inc. All rights reserved.

What happened? Was there an unexpected surge in demand for what we were offering? We didn't see any signs of that in the market. However, I believe the increase was due to our customers' *perception* that our higher prices meant higher value. Because customers are generally willing to pay more for higher quality and value, it follows that they often believe there is higher quality and value when there is a higher price—even when the true value is the same. (By the way, to take advantage of the additional and highly profitable workload, as well as create more time with our families, we recruited and trained more consultants.) See Figure 2.11.

Market Position 3: Offer Customers Less and Charge Them More

You may be wondering whether this scenario would ever take place, but it actually happens all the time. There may even be

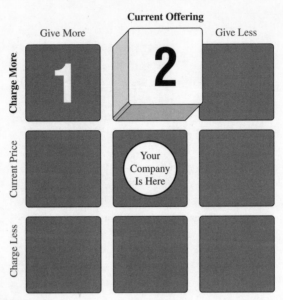

Figure 2.11

The More or Less Value Model, © 2010 by More or Less, Inc. All rights reserved.

circumstances where this strategy *should* be implemented in your company. Let's say you have a handful of customers who are more trouble than they are worth—both emotionally and financially. Perhaps they are abusive or unreasonably demanding. In these situations, you could refuse to do business with them, or you could value the relationship appropriately by raising their prices while reducing what you offer them. They may stay with you, or they may leave. Either way, you're happy.

Here's another reason why you might charge more and deliver less: Sometimes, less is more. Do your offerings have more bells, whistles, features, and benefits than customers want or need? All this extra fluff might actually be getting in the way—and it happens more often than we like to admit. Because you know and understand your products and services completely (and fully appreciate them), you think your customers should, too. But sometimes, they don't. Instead, they buy from you *in spite* of the extra features, not because of them. Could you offer a simpler—and therefore more useful—product or service and charge more for the luxury of simplicity? If you don't, your competitor may. Look at your offerings and see.

Some companies really are charging more and giving less; only now, they're doing it in volume. If you're the kind of shopper who reads labels and calculates the price per ounce in bulk food packages, you have likely found many bulk products that actually cost *more* per unit than when they are sold in smaller quantities. Shoppers assume that buying the mega multifamily, super-sized package of a given product will get them the lowest per-unit price, but that is less so these days. See Figure 2.12.

Figure 2.12

Market Position 4: Offer More for the Same Price

This is a good way to keep customers if you can do it. Cost efficiencies can help a company offer more for the same price, but it's a depressing pathway if driven by market or competitive pressures. When an increasing number of competitors enter a given market, a march toward commoditization begins. Commoditization is when your product or service is in the process of becoming a commodity, or a common "me too" offering. When this takes place, the particular product or service has less perceived value. Consequently, customers will expect more and more over time for the same price. Sadly, this trend is difficult to reverse unless you can find a way to differentiate your offering from others in your market. If you see your company heading in this direction, be creative in making your offering more valuable or appealing.

Think of water as an example of this. Is there any product more common than water? It should be one of the cheapest products on the planet, but it has been expertly differentiated. In fact, customers pay as much as $18 per gallon of "high-quality" bottled spring water. Even the cheaper brands—which consist mainly of filtered tap water—sell for around $1 per gallon. This is insanity; consumers are paying from $1 to $18 for something that flows from their faucets at home for virtually *no* cost! If water can be rescued from commoditization through creative differentiation, then your products or services can, too. Some ways to distinguish a commodity from its rivals are upgraded packaging, value-added services, and selling it together with another product. Creativity is always the key to differentiation. If you can propose ways to transform your customers' perception of your offerings' value, you will improve your employer's perception of your *own* value at the same time. See Figure 2.13.

Figure 2.13

The More or Less Value Model, © 2010 by More or Less, Inc. All rights reserved.

Market Position 6: Offer Less at the Same Price

This tactic has been widely adopted by manufacturers recently. Smaller food portions at grocery stores and fast-food chains, bars of soap with 12 percent less mass, and "half-gallon" cartons of ice cream containing only one and a half quarts all exemplify offering less of a product for the same price. The manufacturers' gamble in reduction is that brand loyalty will compel customers' continued purchases. After all, the food tastes just as good, the soap smells just as clean and fresh, and the ice cream is just as creamy as its larger counterpart was. Frankly, most people don't even notice a companies' shrinking value propositions, and if they do, often customer loyalty does, in fact, win out.

Can your company continue to provide an acceptable yet somehow lesser offering to your customers in an effort to maintain

Figure 2.14

your bottom line? You may not have this option, depending on your industry and the product or service you provide. However, it is worth exploring, especially if your competition is offering less for the same. This strategy is similar to position 2 but more subtle; it keeps the price the same and diminishes the offering rather than raising prices on a current offering. See Figure 2.14.

Market Position 7: Give More and Charge Less

Commoditization! If your company is being pushed into this negative market position, your customers probably view your products or services as absolute commodities. If you were worried that you were heading in this direction while in position 4, position 7 indicates that you have indeed arrived. And chances are your competition is also there. Often, opponents who battle it out in this arena experience razor-thin profit margins, with little or no ability to weather an economic downturn without a strong

Balance Sheet. Here, your pricing is set not as much by your choice as by the common price at which many others are selling. To profitably remain in this position, your company must either find a way to add substantial value to customers over and above your core product/service or dominate the market as one of the largest, highest volume players.

There is a strategic—if sinister—reason to deliberately give more and charge less than anyone else in your market. If a company with a strong enough Balance Sheet is trying to gain market share by eliminating competition, it can sustain large P&L losses while others suffer and eventually go out of business. With fewer competitors, prices can later be raised to profitable levels. This is a natural occurrence in times of economic turmoil, when weaker competitors can't last until an upturn. The strong will survive and gain greater market share as an expected consequence of prolonged market pressures. See Figure 2.15.

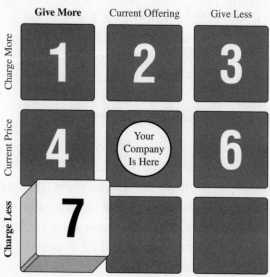

Figure 2.15

The More or Less Value Model, © 2010 by More or Less, Inc. All rights reserved.

Market Position 8: Charge Less for the Same Thing

During a recession—when markets and economies shrink—it is common for sales to stall and inventories to bulge due to falling demand. In other words, people and companies decrease or cease their routine purchasing practices and hold onto their cash. With slowing sales, growing inventories, and scarce cash, it's common to lower prices while keeping offerings the same. This strategy improves a company's value proposition in order to stimulate sales and maintain cash flow. It is similar to what is done in market position 4, but lowering the price is more visible and often perceived as being more valuable than getting more for the same price.

At times, companies may lose money in position 8, because they have to sell off inventory below their cost. However, it is still a sound decision if the company needs cash to continue meeting payroll and other immediate obligations. The cash previously paid for the inventory is, at this point, "sunk" cost, meaning that cash is gone forever. When the need for cash today is stronger than the desire to make a profit on existing inventory, the move to position 8 makes sense. See Figure 2.16.

Market Position 9: Give Less and Lower the Price

Customers tend to believe that if a company is going to reduce any offering, it should also reduce the price. Conversely, when customers get the benefit of a price decrease, they are generally willing to accept some reduction in what they receive. Can your company fortify its value proposition by announcing—with a lot of fanfare—a price reduction that will be appealing to customers while (quietly) decreasing what you give customers in return? Ideally, you will want to trim product size, quantity, features, or service components that have the least perceived value for

Figure 2.16

The More or Less Value Model, © 2010 by More or Less, Inc. All rights reserved.

customers and provide the highest cost savings for your company. See Figure 2.17.

Value Proposition Summary

As you might guess, making any of the positioning moves shown in the More or Less Value Model will have either positive or negative financial consequences for your organization. Any change in position will cause revenue and expenses to either increase, decrease, or remain the same, which will in turn affect the bottom line and should be carefully considered. For example, if you are looking into a specific value proposition change—such as a move from your current practice to position 6—you would first want to know that expenses would go down and revenue would remain the same, for a net-positive impact to your

Figure 2.17

The More or Less Value Model, © 2010 by More or Less, Inc. All rights reserved.

company's bottom line. For the positive or negative result of each position, see Figure 2.18.

If you look at the net impact of each position, you will quickly notice that—from a profit standpoint—your company will always want to move to 3 and avoid 7. The next most obvious choices would be moves to 2 or 6 while avoiding 4 and 8. We can't immediately know the outcomes of 1 and 9, because we must first analyze how much revenue is increasing relative to the increase in expenses in 1 and how much the revenue is decreasing relative to the decrease in expenses in 9. Both 1 and 9 have the potential to be net positive, net negative, or neutral.

It is important to keep in mind that this model portrays the results of each position on the company's P&L—which is only a part of the total picture. Before any change should be made in a value proposition, other critical factors must be

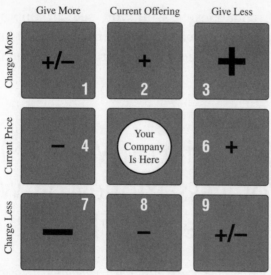

Figure 2.18

The More or Less Value Model, © 2010 by More or Less, Inc. All rights reserved.

studied. For example, when revenue and expense implications are joined with customer intentions, competitors' positions, and market conditions, only then will powerful strategies for sustainable profit generation emerge. The most successful organizations are several moves ahead of their competition when it comes to making deliberate moves to new value propositions to the benefit of their P&L Statements. Less-successful companies are pushed unwillingly into reactive—and negative—positions by customers, markets, and competitors.

If you can help your company be more proactive with its market positioning, you will add incredible and uncommon value. As you see your company making difficult changes in products, services, and pricing that most employees don't understand, you should view those changes through this value proposition filter. This will allow you to recognize and support initiatives that may be critical to the success—and perhaps even survival—of your business. If you see an opportunity for improving your firm's value proposition through an approach that others don't yet recognize, you should immediately propose it.

Should You Work More for Less Money or Work Less for More?

"Most people work just hard enough not to get fired and get paid just enough money not to quit."
—*George Carlin*

Remember my suggestion that you are truly a business unit of one? Let's assume that you are the president of your own company and you have only one customer: your employer. You should consider your personal value proposition to your employer; you might be able to improve it for both of you. See Figure 2.19.

You are currently selling your services to your employer for a certain price. This pay arrangement for services is your *value proposition* to your company. Now is the time to ask some important questions. Should you continue to offer the same services for the same pay, or is there a better value proposition? Is the existing deal still working for you and your employer, or can it be improved?

As we just learned, outside forces can change the relationship between your company and its customers. These changes are inevitable and require modifications in your company's value proposition. Likewise, you need to assess similar changes in *your*

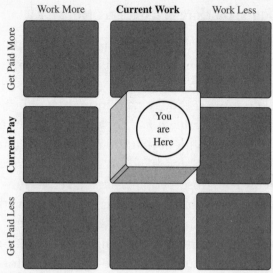

Figure 2.19

The More or Less Employment Model, © 2010 by More or Less, Inc.
All rights reserved.

relationship with your employer. You may have been hired when
unemployment was low and the economy was soaring. Have
these factors stayed the same, or have they changed? You may not
have had much experience or education when you started to work
with your current employer. Have you since earned an advanced
degree or become an expert in your field? The fact is that you
may be more or less needed by your company and more or less
employable in the open market. A review of your personal value
proposition will bring your attention to options that can make
you generally more employable—and more needed by your
company, specifically.

If change is forcing you out of your current value proposition, what is your new value destination? Just as there are for your
company, there are eight other value positions for you to personally explore aside from your current value position. Several of
those alternatives could work for both you and your employer.
Let's examine them now.

Career Position 1: Do More and Get Paid More for It

Having interviewed, hired, and managed many employees over the years, I have observed two distinct employee attitudes regarding compensation. The first type embraces the outlook that they will do more if they're paid more first. The second type will demonstrate their value *before* they expect a commitment for more pay. They are confident that they will be paid more because of the value they know they can add. You can guess that for every 100 employees I've observed, perhaps five fit into the latter category. There's nothing particularly *wrong* with wanting more money before you do more work; it's surely an understandable perspective, and I'm not faulting anyone for having it. But the prior demonstration of above-average performance at a well-run company usually leads to significant raises, bonuses, recognition, and promotions. Truly indispensable workers don't even work for the money. While compensation is important and necessary to them, indispensable employees will do more than they are paid to do, because they're working to gain additional skills, knowledge, and experience. They know that what they learn will be worth more money long term than whatever their immediate paycheck brings. And while working for the experience may sound altruistic, it isn't. It's actually a quicker way to higher compensation than waiting to get more pay before giving more work. In fact, you could even view additional, uncompensated work as blatantly self-interested.

Remember my story about my experience as a machinist? Like every starving college student, I *really* was starving. When I got the machinist job and was told what the pay would be, I realized that it would not cover my expenses. But because I had no other employment offers, I decided to take the job and make the best of it. I asked the personnel manager when employees usually received raises and how much the first raise might be. He replied that I shouldn't expect a raise before six months—probably more like a year. He also informed me that although I *might* receive as much as $0.50, it would most likely be $0.10 per hour. This was devastating news. Out of desperation, I half-jokingly proposed that if after 30 days he was absolutely thrilled with the work I was doing, he should consider giving me a $1-per-hour raise. He laughed.

After working for a while—a time during which I corrected the inefficient process and machine configuration (when the president came down to the production floor to personally thank me for the increased productivity)—the personnel manager called me into his office. It was the thirtieth day of my employment. He told me I got the $1 raise—and informed me that if I told anyone about it, he would kill me. Because he was smiling, it seemed unlikely he would have actually killed me, but I kept the secret, anyway.

And now you know "the secret": Do more *before* you receive more compensation. Give unexpected value, and *then* expect something good in return. Knock your employer's socks off, and watch what happens. Although the lesson I learned from my machinist work came not from my intelligence but rather from my desperation, it has established a pattern of job performance for me and yielded many wonderful financial benefits in my career. See Figure 2.20.

Career Position 2: Get More Money Doing Your Current Job

More pay for the same work is common in most organizations. In recent years, pay raises have averaged around 3.8 percent.[11] Your industry average may vary slightly, but you have probably experienced annual raises without having to perform beyond your job description. However, there are a couple of problems for employees who rely on automatic raises to improve their standard of living. First, inflation—which has run at about 2.7 percent[12]—eats up most of the pay raise, leaving no

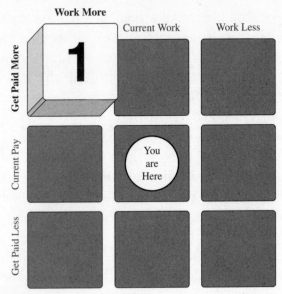

Figure 2.20

The More or Less Employment Model, © 2010 by More or Less, Inc.
All rights reserved.

noticeable net increase. Second, in difficult economic times, some companies don't increase pay at all. If you want to benefit both yourself and your employer by moving to position 2, there is a better vehicle than the annual raise.

The best way to take advantage of career position 2 is to propose cost-cutting and revenue-generating ideas to your company. While performing all of your usual tasks in your job description, use any of the ideas in Part 2, along with the Profit Proposal Generator at our web site (www.indispensablebymonday.com), to turn your best thinking into profit-producing reality. The nice thing about this process is that you don't have to do the work of implementing your proposals; the company will do it for you. A solid profit proposal from you has tremendous value in and of itself.

So, how will your great ideas translate into increased pay for you? Many companies will have an incentive pay program that is designed to reward all implemented proposals. Some companies

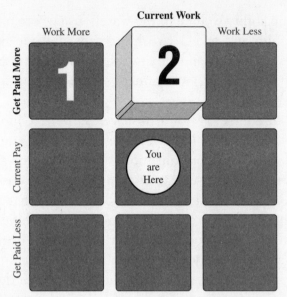

Figure 2.21

The More or Less Employment Model, © 2010 by More or Less, Inc. All rights reserved.

will pay a percentage of the net benefit a proposal produces, while others offer trips, paid time off, or any number of similar rewards. Of course, you'll receive a larger, long-term benefit: an enhanced resume and a better chance of getting a promotion or another job offer, both of which would probably mean substantially more compensation. See Figure 2.21.

Career Position 3: Get Paid More to Do Less

This position is clearly the most highly prized. The challenge is finding a way to make it happen. Here's an example of how one person tried it. Once, while interviewing workers at a major automobile manufacturer, we asked the question, "Who is a hero around here?" The response was unanimous and loud: "Vern! Yeah, Vern's the man!" We asked what it was about Vern that made him a champion in their minds. It turns out that Vern had the awesome ability to hide in the warehouse where no manager could find him and take a two-hour nap any time he wanted. He was never caught, and he always maxed out on his annual bonus. As consultants, we gained some interesting cultural insights that day.

Vern, of course, is not a positive example. Unfortunately, some employees will take advantage of trusting employers in order to do less and get paid more. But we're not aiming for mediocrity at the expense of your company. If you want to move to position 3, you should attempt to do it in a way that also works for your company. For example, you might combine the cost-cutting and revenue-producing practices you are learning here with a more efficient way of doing your job. The combination of these two efforts will actually reduce your workload while providing an opportunity for increased pay. Enhancing your personal efficiency to make your job easier is the strategy found in position 6 (do less for the same pay). Combine position 6 (to be discussed) with the strategy of position 2, and your cumulative efforts will get you into position 3—where you *really* want to be. See Figure 2.22.

Career Position 4: Do More for the Same Pay

When an employer asks a worker to do more without an increase in pay, things can get a little dicey. Employees can feel violated and abused in these situations. Perhaps there have been recent layoffs that have piled more work onto the remaining staff members. If you're pushed into this uncomfortable position, what can you do? You have some options. You could justifiably gripe and complain, or you could recognize the circumstances for what they are—hard times for the company. Personally, I see this as a chance to be more positive than those around you, reduce costs and increase revenue to the best of your ability, and become indispensable in every way possible. The tough times may only be temporary, or you may find yourself and your

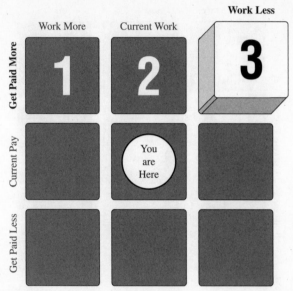

Figure 2.22

The More or Less Employment Model, © 2010 by More or Less, Inc.
All rights reserved.

coworkers rapidly heading into position 7 (more work and less pay)—which makes position 4 look like a picnic. Either way, you come out of the ordeal with a stronger resume, more experience, and greater employability. Whether with your current company in the future or in a different job, you win. This type of positive outlook and proactive behavior will enable you to establish yourself as a must-keep candidate if more pink slips start to fly, and you will find that life is just plain better when you are doing things that are constructive in an otherwise chaotic atmosphere. See Figure 2.23.

Career Position 6: Do Less and Get Paid the Same

One of my jobs as a teenager was plastering swimming pools in southern California. It was my job to haul the crew's tools and equipment into the backyard before construction began. Then, I had to break open and empty 100-pound bags of sand and

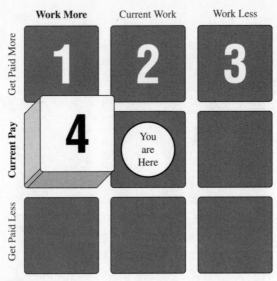

Figure 2.23

cement into a large cement mixer on the back of a very big truck. That was the easy part of my physical labor. Next, I had to push 350-pound wheelbarrow loads to the pool. Then, I had to scoop 50-pound shovelfuls of cement from the wheelbarrow down onto the walls of the pool from the deck above. The average pool required more than 1.5 tons of white cement to be shoveled by hand. My coworkers and I completed two pools a day, which, after my calculations, amounted to hand shoveling *three tons* of cement per day. When the shoveling was finished, I hauled all those tools, shovels, trowels, and other stuff back to the truck again. Throughout the course of the job, there was a lot of back and forth, up and down, and running around. I seemed to be constantly fetching cement or tools from the truck to the site or vice versa. Also, the truck bed holding the mixer sat high in the air, and I remember the pain caused by the exhaustive climbing up and jumping down from that bed, most often with full and heavy loads. Are you feeling sorry for me yet?

I was paid a set amount of money per pool. While doing the job faster wouldn't earn me any more money, doing it slower would get me fired. The problem was, with the physical movement that was necessary, I couldn't figure out how to accomplish everything in the time available without having a near-death experience. This job was killing me. I was being run ragged by all the trips between the truck on the street and the pool in the backyard, again and again. I asked others in the company in my same position if they were experiencing the same challenges, and they all were. It was a grunt job at the very bottom of the pool-plastering work crew. If I had to do it today, I would be hospitalized within 20 minutes. But I'm glad I did it—because it taught me how to work less for a fixed paycheck.

Looking back at it now, it seems so simple: The solution was to maximize every single trip to and from the pool. Upon learning this, I never again wasted an opportunity to transport the maximum load. So, when the foreman wanted me to run out to the truck to get one small item, I maximized the opportunity to load the wheelbarrow with any items that were no longer needed at the pool site and transport them to the truck. Once at the truck, I'd grab the foreman's item and load anything else we may have needed for my return trip. By so doing, I minimized the total number of trips, which saved a lot of time and energy. My pay remained the same per pool, but the energy and time spent performing my job was drastically reduced. It became as manageable as a job that requires the shoveling of over three tons of cement per day could possibly be. Ah, to be 18 again! Luckily for plastering crews today, they have pump trucks and hoses; no more shoveling from wheelbarrows.

There are most likely similar opportunities to eliminate wasted time and streamline your efforts in your own position. Think of the hours you spend in inefficient meetings, conversations, and "trips" within your office or facility. There are many ways to do less for the same pay if you cut out activities that

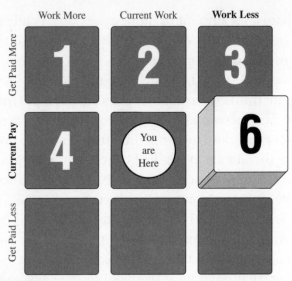

Figure 2.24

The More or Less Employment Model, © 2010 by More or Less, Inc.
All rights reserved.

don't get work done and keep those that *do*. If you informally review where you spend your time and then exercise a little self-discipline, you will most likely stop running yourself ragged and get your real work done. And keep in mind that frantic activity does not equal high productivity. See Figure 2.24.

Career Position 7: Do More for Your Company and Get Paid Less

Well, this is it—the bottom of the employment barrel. If you've been squeezed into this position, your company is likely experiencing a serious cash crunch and it may have laid off about all of the personnel it can and still operate. You and your remaining coworkers are feeling the strain of doing your own job as well as all or part of someone else's job. And that pay cut didn't help matters, either. If the employment market is solid, you have considered leaving your company for greener pastures. In your more optimistic moments, you might be tempted to think of the bright side—that less pay is better than no pay, and long hours spent at work are better than long hours spent looking for work. Overall, this is not a pretty picture. So, what can you do in this situation?

Believe it or not, things are not as bleak as they may seem. In fact, this is the time when people can most easily become indispensable. Helping your company with profit-enhancing ideas in these dire circumstances is more valuable than anything you might propose during a healthier financial time. So, carry the workload, take the pay cut, and find extra money by any means possible to help your employer survive. The company will implement more of what you propose in such a situation, and your resume will begin to make you look like a real magician for contributing unexpected dollars to your employer. Even if your company does eventually go out of business, it will be easier for you to get another—and perhaps better—job at a different company if you have something like the following on your resume:

> *During the last six months before Deadco went out of business and while morale was at its lowest among the remaining workforce, I proposed five cost-cutting and income-increasing measures that provided $28,000 in unexpected cash. Had the company continued operations, these contributions would have totaled $140,000 in net profit over five years, which would have been equal to the profit from $2 million in sales.*

Now, I ask you: What kind of weight will this carry in your next job interview? You will be regarded as one who refuses to surrender to negative forces, even if everyone else does. It will be obvious to a prospective employer that you will fight for your company, even in the toughest of circumstances. You will

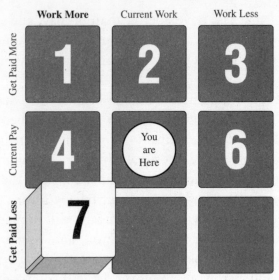

Figure 2.25

have a serious edge over other applicants and will be recognized as indispensable. See, even position 7 has its benefits. See Figure 2.25.

Career Position 8: Get Paid Less for the Same Work

After the bleak scenario we just reviewed in position 7, the situation at position 8 feels like a walk in the park. Of course, a pay cut is never a good thing, and it's certainly a sign of financial stress for your company. This situation is similar to position 4, except the company has chosen in position 8 to keep more workers at less pay rather than retain fewer workers at the same pay levels. As always, in position 8, the option to be proactive and contribute to the bottom line is your best alternative. Once an uncommon practice, keeping more people employed but at fewer hours and for less pay has become a strategy of choice for struggling companies. The positive message in this otherwise

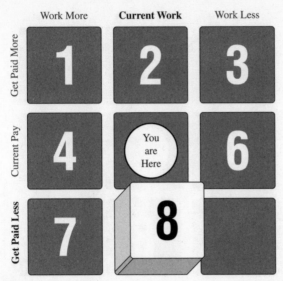

Figure 2.26

The More or Less Employment Model, © 2010 by More or Less, Inc.
All rights reserved.

negative situation is that the company is trying to *keep more people employed*. See Figure 2.26.

Career Position 9: Less Work for Less Pay

This represents a lifestyle change that could have some appeal to a number of people in the workplace. Cutting back on hours and responsibilities—even working from home—might be a break-even proposition when one considers the expenses related to full-time employment. Position 9 might even be more like position 6 when you examine it closely. If your company is experiencing financial pressure and it becomes necessary to cut your hours—and if you can spend more work time and time off at home—would the cost of things like your daily commute, child care, yard work, and meals go down? Would you spend less on your wardrobe? If you add up all the money you would save by being home more and working less, could that total reduction in expenses be about equal

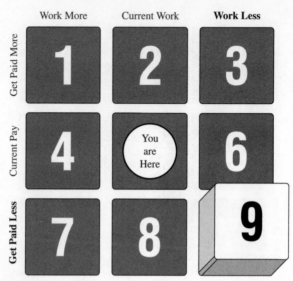

Figure 2.27

The More or Less Employment Model, © 2010 by More or Less, Inc. All rights reserved.

to your reduction in income? There could also be an increase in your quality of life as you begin enjoying more personal and family time and less job stress. See Figure 2.27.

Your Personal Value Proposition Summary

As you have discovered, making any of the positioning moves we've discussed will result in financial and workload consequences—some positive and some negative—for you and your company. With every position, both income and obligation can increase, decrease, or remain the same. These outcomes will always have an impact on you and should be carefully considered when any change is explored. For the positive or negative result of each position, see Figure 2.28.

It's apparent when looking at the net effect of each position that most people would want to move to 3, 2, or 6. It would also be wise to avoid 7, 4, and 8 if possible. Positions 1 and 9 may have

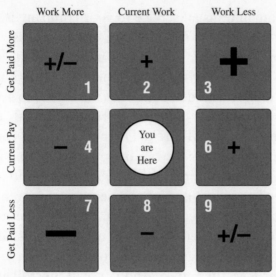

Figure 2.28

The More or Less Employment Model, © 2010 by More or Less, Inc.
All rights reserved.

net benefits, but more analysis is required to determine the actual outcome.

Might there ever be a time when you would voluntarily and strategically choose to move into position 7, 4, or 8, or do people only go there kicking and screaming? If you ever start noticing signs that your company is experiencing financial stress—such as a strained P&L, tight economy, and layoffs—and if you can anticipate that your company will have no choice but to start moving workers into positions 7, 4, and 8, you could in fact volunteer to make a move in this direction *before* it becomes mandatory. Asking for more responsibility (position 4), suggesting a temporary pay cut for yourself (position 8), or doing both (position 7) can show that you are not only aware of the business problems your company is facing but that you are also willing to be a part of the solution. Volunteering for that which is going to happen before it even takes place can be a wise strategy, and spending time in unusual service to your company is sometimes the same as paying your dues. In other words, temporary residency in position 7, 4, or 8 can be your most direct route to position 3, 2, or 6 when better financial conditions return.

Please don't misunderstand what I'm trying to say here; I'm not pretending that your company will always directly reward you for your efforts described herein. I know that even if you become a superhuman contributor to your organization, you could still be laid off because of your hiring date and lack of seniority. You might still be passed over for promotions because of entrenched company politics, and your employer might not be able to weather a financial storm. However, if you give more, get less, and have no expectation for immediate reward, you will be on your way to greater rewards in the future. And you will most likely be compensated in the near term, anyway. If you can take anything on faith, take this. Just remember to document all contributions in your resume so that they *can* come back to you with greater value.

> *"Folks who never do any more than they get paid*
> *for, never get paid for any more than they do."*
> —Elbert Hubbard

 Profit Source **14**   # Soft Skill, Solid Results

If you read current books (other than this one) and blogs about becoming indispensable at work, you will most often be advised to remain loyal, leave your personal life at home, check your ego at the door, improve your appearance, give your best, be nice, make yourself useful, be "visible," and so forth. You have by now figured out that my opinion in this area is simple: Your job is to add real value to your customers and company, and that value should be directly measurable in dollars.

Naturally, you'll want to do so in a professional and pleasant manner and perform your job such that your coworkers and customers are comfortable around you and want to continue working with you. If you become a star in the area of profit enhancement but are intolerable to team members and customers, your manager may lock you in your office. On the other hand, if everyone prefers to work with you over anyone else in the entire organization, but you fail to produce anything of value, your job could be at risk. Your challenge, then, is to increase your business value and make progress interpersonally at the same time. (Please bear in mind that I am not talking about the limp list in the previous paragraph.)

What if there was *one* interpersonal skill that not only made you more pleasant to those around you but also increased your ability to accomplish the hard-dollar strategies that we've been exploring? As luck would have it, there is such a soft skill, and it yields very solid results. To the extent you can master it, the world will literally open up to you as never before. That skill is interpersonal communication.

But how does this particular ability yield dollars? Well, for one thing, it's certainly easier to successfully implement a profit-producing proposal when you have above-average communication ability. You will navigate a tense situation with a customer more smoothly if you can connect well with others, and you'll exhibit just the right mix of assertiveness and deference in a performance appraisal and quickly enlist the help of coworkers with your next time-sensitive project if you can interface well with other carbon-based life forms. Conflict resolution, negotiation, and motivation of others all depend greatly upon your communication abilities. Teamwork, leadership, and meeting management will soar if you master this skill.

So, how are you as a communicator? Everyone can be ranked on an imaginary competency scale somewhere between, *"It's best if you just keep your pie hole shut,"* and *"You're the only one in the company who can give this presentation."* You and I probably fall somewhere in the middle of that scale. When we're with people we know and trust—and when the conversation is not serious—we dialogue pretty well. But those aren't the situations where communication can make or break a customer relationship, career, or marriage. We need to exhibit our best skill when things get the rockiest between ourselves and others. Good communication skills count most when we are embroiled in stressful conversations

Having (hopefully) made the case for why you should consider upgrading your communication abilities—especially in difficult situations—I am not going to attempt to teach you *how* to do so. That would be well beyond the scope of this book. Besides, that book has already been written, and I want to recommend it to you now. It is called *Crucial Conversations*. It was written by my former partners, Kerry Patterson, Joseph Grenny, Ron McMillan, and Al Switzler, and if you should get your hands on it, I hope the concepts you find and the abilities you gain by studying it will change your life in the same wonderful ways they have changed mine. When I discussed earlier the benefits you can enjoy by soaking up the concentrated information of great authors of nonfiction books, *Crucial Conversations* is exactly the type of knowledge I was referring to.

To recap: Don't just be an employee who brings a lot of unexpected profit to your company, and don't just be an expert in interpersonal communication. Be both—and you will be indispensable. This skill is the intangible portion of the assets on your personal Balance Sheet, and intangible assets provide the capacity to make money. You will increase your ability to add financial value—to yourself and your employer—by developing your communication prowess.

PART III

Making It All Work . . . Starting Monday Morning

Now that you are trained in the basics of profit making, and you have learned how to generate high impact profit proposals, it's time to refine your approach so that you can gain the maximum benefit from these newly acquired skills. There are additional considerations that will help you succeed.

You should get the most career mileage out of every one of your profit ideas. Some profit opportunities should be pursued, others should be postponed, and still others must be ignored altogether. Further, if you're in sales or management there are special techniques that could help you even more. Part 3 provides the expertise you need in order to maximize the benefits you will create for your company and for yourself.

Problem Solving: Generate Only the Highest Value Solutions

Here's something your manager wants you to know: No employee is more highly valued than the one who takes on and solves problems, and no employee is a bigger pain in the neck than the one who is regularly overwhelmed by them. Being able to deal with job-related challenges is a skill that every worker who expects to stay employed—not to mention move up in the organization— must master. However, it is only the beginning of a broader capability you are required to develop in order to become indispensable. Responding to challenges that come your way in the normal course of your job is a good thing that you should definitely do well; but at times, you will also need to look outside your job to solve problems that no one else can even see yet. In other words, you will need to seek out the hidden problems that are sacrificing your company's profit, either in the form of costs that can be cut or revenue that can be captured. This is, of course, the main focus of everything we have discussed so far.

Every example of increased profit about which you have read here has come as a solution to a problem, and every resume entry I have shown you represents a solution to a problem. In fact, some of your resume could logically be under the heading, "Profit-Enhancing Solutions." Instead, we most often use the traditional heading, "Work Experience." Maybe it's time to change the format of our resumes. To show the link between business problems and their profit-enhancing solutions, let's randomly choose a few of the resume entries we have already seen and view them again, but this time with the corresponding business challenges that gave rise to them.

Problem: The company was doing some work for which it was not invoicing its clients.

Solution:
Developed an innovative process for accurately capturing legitimate billing opportunities that were being missed by the company. During the first year of implementation, the process resulted in invoicing over $150,000 in additional revenue that would have been otherwise lost. This bottom-line contribution is equal to the profit earned by the company on a $5 million contract.

Problem: The company was faced with either cost cuts or layoffs.

Solution:
Established a new system for contacting each customer to let them know their order was complete and ready to ship. During each customer contact, a simple option was offered regarding shipping preference. They could either get three-day shipping for free or higher-priority delivery service, which they would

pay for. Customers chose to pay for faster delivery 20 percent of the time, reducing our shipping costs by $12,500 per year. This is the same amount of profit produced by $178,571 in product sales. An unexpected benefit of this innovation was the enhanced service our customers felt they were receiving due to the added contact, as at times, we updated shipping addresses and other incorrect customer information.

Problem: A lot of solid potential customers were ready and willing to buy but couldn't get financing.

Solution:
After numerous customers complained about their inability to get financing for the purchase of our product, I proposed an in-house financing service for qualified buyers. This new service was immediately profitable due to our interest rate, and it increased product sales by $2.6 million annually. To keep up with our increase in sales, my company purchased more raw materials from our suppliers, entitling us to supplier discounts in the amount of $64,500. Savings from discounts alone generated the same amount of profit as would have been generated by $921,428 in product sales.

As you can see, you create profit for your company—and gain a killer resume—by first tackling significant problems. In other words, problems are your friends. They really are blessings in disguise. Without them and the money they cost your company, you would have nothing to propose or implement in the way of profit-producing solutions.

However, most people want their lives to be easy. They think they will enjoy their jobs more if there are no tough issues to deal with at work; but they need to think differently. Of course, most never will, which makes this your opportunity to stand up and *be* different. If your goal is to have a trouble-free existence at work, you will probably try to avoid any problem that comes your way. If, on the other hand, your goal is to increase your employability—and receive all of the benefits that come with being more valuable—you will almost *pray* for problems. You will take them on wherever you can find them, whether they're part of your normal job description or you discover them elsewhere in the company.

If you have decided to become a problem-solver extraordinaire, the next questions are how to determine which challenges to work on first and if you should even work on a given problem at all. To address these issues, I would like to introduce a simple model that can help you determine how to handle each profit opportunity you encounter (see Figure 3.1). It helps you understand how to approach a problem by exploring two basic issues: first, the amount of profit your company would realize from a potential solution of the target problem; and second, the possibility of you actually being able to implement the solution.

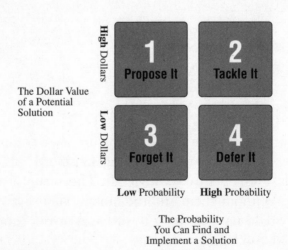

Figure 3.1

If successful, Quadrants 1 and 2 will be resume entries, because they bring substantial financial value to your employer. While both will go a long way toward increasing your personal value and employability, Q2 is where you should spend most of your problem-solving energy, since you will be credited with implementing the solution, not just proposing that the problem be analyzed as in Q1. An alternate plan for a Q1 problem would be to team up with the right people and work on it together. However, if you aren't comfortable doing this, then submitting a proposal is the next best thing.

Quadrant 3 is where many people will apply their problem-solving efforts. This is a waste of time. Once you determine that solving a particular problem brings little financial benefit to the company—and that you probably can't do much to fix it, anyway—run. Finally, Quadrant 4 is where you park the small- to medium-dollar projects until you have temporarily run out of Q1 and Q2 targets. Quadrant 4 problems are back-burner challenges that are only worth working on when you have nothing better to do, so postponing them is a good idea.

Now that you have a way to prioritize problems, you'll never again find yourself dealing with low-value initiatives. Leave those to other, less-productive people. Spend your time focusing on the areas that will bring real value to your company and positive attention to yourself.

The New and Improved Performance Appraisal

Performance appraisal, performance management, performance review, performance rating—call it what you will, it just doesn't work. You know it, and I know it. The system is open to manipulation, is too subjective, and chews up too much time and money; employees and supervisors alike dread it. In most cases, it's even counterproductive, causing negative feelings and a depressed culture that saps productivity. Do you want to contribute some real money to the bottom line? Obliterate your performance appraisal system. That's right: Wipe it out, destroy it, demolish it, eliminate it, eradicate it, annihilate it, and reduce it to nothing. If my thesaurus had more synonyms, I would have gladly used them. Performance management as we commonly practice it obscures the very thing we should be measuring in individuals while perpetuating countless non-value-added behaviors throughout the organization.

If the performance appraisal's primary goal is to align employees' actions with the mission of the company—and measure that alignment—then we must first ask what the mission of the company is. The company's mission (at its core) is to earn more money than it spends, remember? The company itself is measured via its Profit and Loss Statement and Balance Sheet. If we really want to align the organization and its employees, we will establish a completely objective set of employee measures that mirror the company's. It follows that each employee should have a P&L and Balance Sheet that track their individual financial contributions; now *that* would be alignment of the highest order.

Alas, this is a hollow dream for the vast majority of companies who are so set in their managerial ways that they may never escape the gravity of the dysfunction that is the performance appraisal. However, there are things you can do to transform your own appraisal from a purely subjective supervisory assessment to a much more objective acknowledgment of your financial contributions to the business. Before your next review, gather the following items:

- *Your personal P&L Statement* showing the money you have earned and cost the company during the previous year

- *Your personal Balance Sheet* showing tangible assets (such as the future value of your recurring profit innovations) and intangible assets that give you the capacity to bring in more money in the future (such as interpersonal communication skills or an advanced degree)

- *Profit proposals* you have made to the company (implemented or not) and a plan for what you intend to work on in the coming year that will further help the company's finances, including how you will increase your financial role by becoming better at your own job

- *Resume entries* documenting the financial results of your proposals that were implemented since your last appraisal

- Your *0 to 100 Quality Target Scale*, which is Figure 2.4 in Profit Source 7 of Part 2.

Armed with undeniable and objective evidence of your value to the company, you will be prepared to bypass your supervisor's selective and skewed memory of what you did during the past year. Furthermore, you will have a better chance of steering the conversation where it should go, which is the documentation of your actual value to the company. A subjective and inaccurate review will be almost impossible if you follow these instructions. If, on the other hand, you have thoroughly enjoyed your reviews in the past, then disregard this advice altogether.

If You're in Sales, Outsell Everyone Else

Any employee in your company can utilize the strategies in this book. But because of your business development responsibilities, you have direct access to customers—which means that you will have more frequent opportunities in the normal course of your work to implement the profit-producing methods that involve customers. The most important concept to keep in mind as you work with customers is this: *Every customer* must *bring in more money than he or she spends*. You might remember that this is the prime directive that drives business decisions to hire and keep employees. It is the same reasoning behind customers' decisions to choose and continue to buy from providers, especially in business-to-business transactions but also in many consumer purchases. Remaining aware of this critical concern gives you a powerful new way to position your company's products/ services in the minds of prospective and existing customers. Features and benefits are interesting and informative, but you must also showcase the aspects of your offering that will create net-positive financial results for buyers. What are the specific characteristics of your offering that will help your customers bring in more money than they spend? Is it your price? Will your product last longer due to higher quality? Can you deliver faster than the competition? Do you help your customers in ways that the competition does not?

Two partners and I started a commercial photo lab in southern California 20 years ago. This was my second start-up, and—just like every new business—the owners necessarily wore many hats. I fondly remember making sales calls during the day, writing up invoices before going home to dinner, and then coming back to build out the lab at night. In our first month, we did a total of $5,000 in business. By month 18, we were up to $320,000 and climbing. At month 19, we were bought out by the world's largest photo lab.

During that year and a half period, we reached the same sales volume as competing labs that had been in the area for 10 and 15 years. We accomplished this by providing our customers— architects, ad agencies, large corporations—with an extra 24 hours of creativity, which meant more money for them. Because we were able to remove a time-consuming step, our processes took a full day less than our competition, and customers used that time to polish and perfect their site plans, ad campaigns, product photo shoots, and other income-dependent presentation materials. The extra creative time translated directly into more money for our customers, because they were then able to present better and more complete work to *their* customers and prospects. Our turnaround time was simply irresistible to most of our customers, who were always up against deadlines.

You should explore all of the ways in which your offering can help your customers become more profitable, and base your business development approach on those key factors. If you know of potential improvements that might better help customers, propose them to your employer. As you evolve from making sales to helping customers prosper, your income production will increase proportionately.

After changing my approach from an emphasis on product features to documenting quantifiable savings by our past customers, my success rate increased substantially. During the last half of the year, I increased personal sales volume by 10 percent. This was in a difficult economy, where every dollar saved by customers was critical.

While you as a sales professional can and should participate in a wide range of profit improvements for your company, your customer relationships will undoubtedly provide you with the highest leverage pathways to becoming indispensable. To demonstrate this point, look back on some of the profit strategies involving customers:

1. Produce more income from existing customers by seeking out and proposing Area 1.5 strategies (Profit Source 2:

Ansoff Revisited—How to Harvest More Money from Customers).

2. Salvage customers who were put off by your company's mistakes (Profit Source 6: If Mistakes *Do* Get Out the Door, Recover Lost Customers).

3. Learn of customers' needs and competitors' new offerings (Profit Source 7: Print Money at Work by Doing Your Own Job Better).

4. Take advantage of chance or casual encounters with customers to create more revenue (Profit Source 8: How I Spent My Summer Vacation—Finding $500,000 in New Zealand).

5. Share successful profit-enhancement methods with customers (Profit Source 10: Become Indispensable to Customers by Giving *Them* Money).

6. Improve your company's value proposition to its customers (Profit Source 12: Give Your Company an Unexpected Competitive Advantage).

The two most important things you can do to make progress in these six customer-related strategies (and sales in general) are (1) ask questions and (2) listen. The best way to illustrate is to relate what happened to me (as luck would have it) just an hour before I started writing this section.

I was on the phone with a saleswoman who talked my ear off about technical specifications in which I had no interest. I just wanted to buy her product and be done with it. In fact, I didn't even care about her product, but I was extremely interested in how I could use the product to accomplish a very important goal. My underlying objective was all that mattered in my mind. After 30 minutes on the phone with me, she still had no clue what my real intention was, even though I tried to explain it several times. She didn't ask a single question about what I was trying to achieve. I finally ended the call in frustration, without purchasing anything from her.

That scene is played out in countless customer interactions daily. If you want to increase your business development success—and if you plan to leverage your relationships with customers to bring additional profits to your company through the six customer-centered strategies previously referenced—you must discover the primary drivers that are motivating buyers. This requires you to stop pushing for the close and start getting at what really matters to the customer.

Talking too much means you're not listening enough. Fortunately, the act of listening can instantly be triggered by questioning—so *you* are in complete control. Ask the right questions, and your prospects will literally give you everything you need to help them succeed, which happens to be the same everything you need to get the deal and bring revenue to your company. Concentrate more on the asking/listening, and you will get more of the closing/earning. What's more, the rewards will come naturally and comfortably. If you are not feeling natural and comfortable in your client contacts, you are neither asking the right questions nor listening enough. And if you're not listening enough, you're talking too much.

> *"Two ears, one mouth. You do the math."*
> —Anonymous

If You're a Leader, Lead Toward Increased Profits

As you have already figured out, this book is about employee engagement. Leaders have been attempting to capture more of the hearts and minds of workers since Og and his team killed their first mastodon, and for the most part, leaders have failed. Consequently, discretionary effort remains the last frontier of organizational efficiency and profit growth. Companies can no longer look to technology, market dominance and expansion, access to capital, or product innovation to sustain the growth and profitability they once enjoyed. Competition is too tight, and customers are too sophisticated. Traditional resources alone will not propel organizations forward at the pace of the past. To produce the competitive advantage you seek, these legacy assets and practices must now be augmented by a deeper and wider utilization of the *human* resource. If you can tap into your people, you will be accessing a vast store of know-how, ingenuity, experience, goodwill, trust, and loyalty. Don't misunderstand: Employee engagement is not employee exploitation. Employees are savvy; they know an unfair exchange when they see one. If, however, they can understand how giving more of themselves will benefit the company and themselves, they will step up. In fact, employees *want* to be engaged. They deeply desire to be successful in their efforts. They want to be part of a winning team, throw themselves into their work, be given appropriate recognition, and continually develop their knowledge and abilities.

So, what exactly should you engage your personnel to do? You should use them to increase the financial success of the organization, of course. After all, isn't that why you hired them in the first place? Greater financial success will come to any company whose people are using more of their discretionary time and effort to enhance the bottom line—that is, if those people have the proper motivation and ability to accomplish that goal. But most employees, even if motivated, don't have the ability to build profits in new ways, and many leaders don't, either. Therefore, what we most often see is the hiring of long term consultants, or the broad request for employees to come up with some profit-building suggestions, or a contest for the best

Figure 3.2

cost-cutting ideas. While some financial benefits do come from these methods, there is a more comprehensive system, and I want to share it with you now.

There are six discreet sources of influence that when utilized in combination with each other will make any undertaking more likely to succeed. The chance of failure increases in proportion to the number of the influence sources you ignore while implementing a strategy. The model you are about to see can be used to increase the success of any endeavor, but we will use it here for the purpose of fully engaging your employees to increase your bottom line. We begin with two of the six sources of power for better financial strength, as seen in Figure 3.2. This "Six Source Model" is used with the permission of VitalSmarts and can be explored more thoroughly in the book *Influencer: The Power to Change Anything* (Patterson et al.).

Source 1, Personal Motivation, is simple: Your people either want to engage in profit-producing actions or they don't. Personal motivation is the first hurdle to get over when attempting to engage employees. If employees personally enjoy other tasks more or don't like adding value, they will be less inclined to jump in and participate. An upgraded resume, higher employability in the market, and the self-satisfaction with a job well done are all motivators for individuals when deciding if they want to make this type of job-related contribution.

Source 2, Personal Ability, can stop even the most enthusiastic employee from finding hidden profits. If someone really wants to help the company become more profitable (source 1—check) but doesn't know where to start or what to do, then you are missing whatever influence could have come from source 2. In this case, it will be necessary to offer some form of training related to profit enhancement. Many companies' profit searches hit the wall at source 2. When leaders ask everyone to find all the profit enhancements they can, people are most often willing but least often able to comply.

Aside from this leader section, this book is written for general employees at all levels of the company. My goal has been to motivate and enable workers to make substantial and mutually beneficial financial impacts that they might not want to make—or be able to make—without such a guide. Sources 1 and 2 represent the extent to which employees can individually contribute without support from management. However, there are another four sources of influence you are about to discover that will greatly increase employee engagement. In these areas, a simple book for the workforce won't suffice. You—as a leader of a team, division, department, or company—will need to pay close attention to these influence sources if you expect to maximize the dollars your employees could ultimately produce. As we move on to sources 3 through 6, you will see why your role is so important.

Source 3, Social Motivation, comes into play when a worker is excited about increasing profits (source 1) and has the ability to do it (source 2) but starts to get pressure from peers about how uncool it is to suck up to the boss with all this profit garbage. "You're making us look bad. Knock it off," they might say; or, "We're all heading out early today. Leave that profit stuff for later and come with us." Any time coworkers use their influence to discourage someone from working toward a healthier bottom line, you have a source 3 barrier. Your job as a leader is to create a culture in which peers actually pressure each other in ways that increase the motivation to perform the tasks that will improve the company's financial situation. Will profit-enhancement success be a cause of embarrassment or a badge of honor?

Source 4, Social Ability, deals with a person's need to obtain permission, answers, help, work—or anything else necessary to do the job at hand—from others. It could be that a team member has neglected to dig up a customer file as promised, or accounting has not sent the requested billing information. Until the needed cooperation is forthcoming, that ex-customer will not be won back. Whenever others make it so someone can't accomplish the desired business outcome, there is a source 4 obstacle. It is possible, and even common, for team members and other departments to be a support in source 3 but a hindrance in source 4. Leaders can diagnose these problems and put remedies in place to smooth out rough interactions. Don't let logistical hiccups stand in the way of a more profitable business. See Figure 3.3.

Now, let's see what happens when we add the structure of your company to the mix, as shown in sources 5 and 6 (see Figure 3.4).

Source 5, Structural Motivation, is where your organization's formal pay, promotions, recognition, and benefits reside. This is the reward system of your business, and it tells workers in no uncertain terms what the company really values. Want to stifle your quest for additional profit? Easy—just promote the people who never give it any effort, or lay off those who perform admirably in this area. The rest of the workforce will soon get

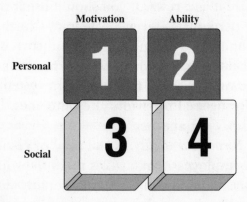

Figure 3.3

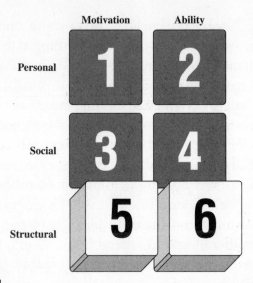

Figure 3.4

the message that finding hidden money is not important, because it's not rewarded—and may even be punished. A certain employee once proposed a cost-cutting measure that resulted in a $200,000 annual (recurring) bottom-line contribution and was given a one-time $500 "thank you." This became a company-wide joke and instantly shut down others' motivation to make further profit efforts for the company. Don't insult your people in this manner. While money is not the only motivator, when you do decide to use it as a reward, you should use it in a measured way that will perpetuate—even proliferate—further successes. Trips, paid time off, recognition, and other rewards can all motivate workers; you get what you pay for. In summary, the organization should align its formal reward system to compensate workers for desired behaviors and outcomes. Don't ask for one thing and pay for another.

Source 6, Structural Ability, is the pool of resources a company provides employees that enables them to properly do their work. Of course, some people cannot properly do their work, because companies do not always provide the right resources to support them. Source 6 includes computer hardware and software, heating and cooling systems, tools, equipment, machinery, budget, raw materials, vehicles, desks, chairs, and conference tables. With regard to increasing profits, what will your company provide employees to enable them to succeed? I know of a controller who was regularly being told by various employees in the company about money-saving ideas. His response was, "That sounds like it could be a good idea, but you need to do some analysis and see if it's feasible. Just get back to me with your projected results." Because most employees had no way of performing such an analysis, they never pursued their ideas to the proposal stage, and the company received no benefit. This is a common problem in many organizations, and it's why we provide a Web-based solution for you to take advantage of. Whenever your people have profit ideas, send them to the Profit Proposal Generator at www.indispensablebymonday.com. With minimal input from them, the system will generate the break-even, sales-equivalency, present-value, and other analyses that will facilitate the selection and implementation of worthwhile initiatives. This is a source 6 solution, and I sincerely hope it supports your efforts. There is no charge for this service, and it should be used to augment any other source 6 tools that you provide your people to enable them to succeed.

Prime the Pump

Here are a few thoughts that could help you direct your work-force. Leaders must prime the pump, so don't automatically shut things down when proposals start coming in. Say yes more than you say no. In the beginning, make a big deal out of people's participation rather than the quantity of dollars generated. Look for the nugget of a workable solution, even when an idea is not a fantastic one; it might become fantastic with some creative tinkering. When you can, use even bad ideas as stepping stones to good ones. By establishing early successes, you will create a positive atmosphere that is more apt to generate additional proposals. Soon, you'll be implementing better proposals, which will produce larger profits, which will invite yet more, superior proposals. Do all in your power to prime the pump of participation and create an upward spiral of success. Never be seen as stealing employees' ideas or being disappointed that you didn't think of it first. Instead, build on good ideas and be part of their implementation when possible. You can be instrumental in transplanting profit innovations to other teams, departments, divisions, or even customers and suppliers. There is always enough glory to go around when incredibly bright ideas are generated.

By conducting several creative sessions with my team, I elicited profit proposals that totaled $125,000 in bottom-line benefits. This profit amount was equal to that produced by $1,785,714 in top-line sales. Of the total profit produced, $68,000 will repeat annually, yielding a sales equivalency of $971,429 each year in the future.

Everything You Need to Know about Accounting—and It's Not Much

A profitable business stands a good chance of surviving, while an unprofitable one does not. Thus, every organization must earn more money than it spends.

Businesses can—and *should*—do much for humanity. Companies should operate under mission/vision statements about serving customers, owners, employees, and other stakeholders. Many businesses generously donate portions of profits to good causes, and many act out of the purest motives for workers' safety and consumers' best interests. Organizations responsibly attempt to shrink their carbon footprints. All are noble and necessary causes; yet, the following fact always remains true.

Every Organization Must Earn More Money Than It Spends.

No organization can continue providing products or services—no matter what benefit they offer to mankind—without making money. Perhaps jaded but entirely accurate is the saying, *"No margin, no mission."*[13] Most leaders, from the CEO on down, are acutely aware of this financial imperative. By becoming more aware of the relentless fiscal fitness needs of your company, you become a more valuable employee. Helping those above you in the organization to meet or exceed their financial numbers is paramount in your quest for indispensability.

What about nonprofit companies? These organizations must operate with the same financial pressure as for-profit companies, but they have their own jargon. Not-for-profit organizations call profit "revenue in excess of expenses" or "net capital." Like their for-profit counterparts, they use excess funds to pay key employee bonuses, hire the best people they can, move into bigger buildings, and buy better copiers; they just don't pay out dividends. Instead, they use all of their profits—or net capital—to invest in, improve, and grow the organization. Nonprofit status normally affords companies some tax advantages. If you work for a nonprofit, you will feel the same performance pressures as workers in any for-profit firm, and you will have the same opportunities to add value and play a significant financial role. So, basically, we *all* need to follow the money. Let's do that now.

Every company tracks dollars coming into and going out of it by way of the Profit and Loss Statement, also called the Income Statement. The P&L is the basic tool for reporting a company's financial situation and the primary indicator of a company's financial performance over time. Creating a P&L is not complicated. First, you show all of the revenue, which is called the "top line," because it appears at the top of the P&L. Next, subtract all of the expenses, below which you either have a positive-net number indicating profit or a negative-net number representing a loss. The net amount—be it positive or negative—is called the "bottom line" because of its obvious position on the P&L. Negative numbers are traditionally shown in parentheses for easy identification. See Figure 3.5.

I'll admit this P&L explanation is somewhat simplified. There are challenges that can affect financial health—even

Profit & Loss Statement Jan. 1 – Dec. 31	
Revenue	
Sales	*$850,000*
Total Revenue	***$850,000***
Expenses	
Salaries	*($650,000)*
Bonuses	*($50,000)*
Insurance	*($75,000)*
Rent	*($25,000)*
Total Expenses	***($800,000)***
Profit (or Loss)	**$50,000**

Figure 3.5

with a positive bottom line—such as cash flow, fast growth, receivable collection time, foreign currency exchange rates, and others. For now, however, let's stick with the basic concept that revenue must exceed expenses and that the P&L is simply a scorecard showing how well your company has performed.

The P&L is backward looking and reports performance during a given period of time (i.e., January 1 to December 31). While financial reports may be prepared in yearly increments, they can also be produced for any time frame—quarterly or monthly, for example. So, management may look at the P&L for a given time period to determine whether the company has been profitable. Profit and Loss Statements can also be created for specific departments or divisions to help leaders understand performance of subcomponents of the company. For example, if a certain geographical subset—say, the northeast division—of the company is outperforming all others, management will want to understand why and attempt to duplicate this financial success company wide. Conversely, if a unit persistently underperforms, management will most likely not stand by patiently and hope for better performance when they know similar units elsewhere are more profitable.

Malaysia Airlines is the perfect example of management using P&Ls to track performance within smaller units of the company.[14] Faced with heavy losses in the company's overall P&L, new CEO Idris Jala, hired in December 2005, wondered why. His curiosity as a newcomer was crucial when he was hired to save the company. So, he instituted a groundbreaking policy that has remarkable implications for other businesses. Jala created subunit P&L Statements to measure each individual flight with its own P&L. Thus, he could readily identify problems and craft solutions more quickly than with only a company-wide financial analysis. As a result, the company could access a staggering 160,000 Profit and Loss Statements as needed. The change that this micro-P&L strategy yielded in

Year	Malaysia Air Profit/(Loss)
2005	($500 million) Loss
2007	$267 million Profit

Figure 3.6

the financial condition of Malaysia Airlines can be seen in Figure 3.6.

The result of Jala's unique viewpoint as a newcomer and the attention to subunit P&Ls restored the company to profit. Is he indispensable? Unquestionably so.

This micro-P&L strategy can be taken even further by creating individual P&L Statements for each employee in the company. This is where it becomes really interesting. What would your personal P&L look like? This important question is explored in great detail in the Part 1 section entitled "Do You Bring in More than You Cost?"

The Balance Sheet

Okay—so your company cannot survive indefinitely if the P&L shows losses; you also need to know about the Balance Sheet. Companies rely on the Balance Sheet to measure financial stability. While the P&L looks at performance over a period of time, the Balance Sheet reflects financial strength on a given day or specific point in time (i.e., as of December 31). In the example I use in Figure 3.7, the assets such as cash, receivables, stocks and bonds, and so forth are listed on the left. The liabilities such as payables, leases, loans, and other payment obligations are listed on the right. The assets minus the liabilities equal the equity—or net worth—of the company.

Have you had enough of the accounting tutorial? There's just a bit more. You're still not ready for that final exam, because

Balance Sheet as of December 31			
Assets		**Liabilities**	
Cash	*$10,000*	*Payables*	*($40,000)*
Receivables	*$30,000*	*Leases*	*($10,000)*
Stocks	*$45,000*	*Loans*	*($25,000)*
Bonds	*$15,000*		
Total		*Total*	
Assets	***$100,000***	*Liabilities*	*($75,000)*
		Equity	*$25,000*

Figure 3.7

you must know how these two measures apply to a company's overall success or failure.

The Good, the Bad, and the Ugly

Let's talk for a moment about clownfish. The clownfish dwells in the poisonous tentacles of the sea anemone. It cleans the anemone, protects it from predators, and is therefore immune from the anemone's poison. In turn, the anemone provides the clownfish with safe refuge from large numbers of predators by shielding the clownfish within its toxic tentacles. It is a relationship of mutual survival and mutual dependence. If either the clownfish or the anemone dies, the other is at risk.

The P&L Statement and the Balance Sheet are similarly related. Separately—although useful in its own way—each individual document does not tell you the full story of the overall financial health of the company. And if either the P&L Statement or the Balance Sheet is suffering, the company can be at risk, even if the other is relatively healthy. If you want to know about the *true* financial health of a company, you must consider both its Balance Sheet and its P&L Statement. (This is a very simplified accounting lesson. There are other accounting considerations affecting a business, but for purposes of our discussion, the big picture of the company's finances is largely depicted with the P&L Statement and Balance Sheet.) The possible relationships between the P&L Statement and the Balance Sheet may be categorized as the good, the bad, and the ugly.

Let's look at the good relationship first. Simply stated, when the P&L reflects consistent profits over multiple periods, the Balance Sheet is typically strong, because the company may use net profit to increase assets, pay down its liabilities, and build equity—or net worth—on the Balance Sheet. See Figure 3.8.

Cash reserves of the company may grow to the level that a for-profit organization will pay dividends to owners rather than retaining and increasing cash reserves indefinitely.

Now let's look at the bad relationship. A financial reservoir of strong assets on the Balance Sheet becomes a lifeline in the event of an economic downturn. Suppose that the company suffers from poor sales performance and records a loss on the

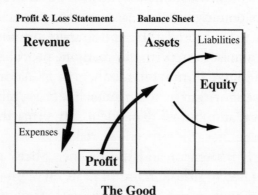

The Good

Figure 3.8

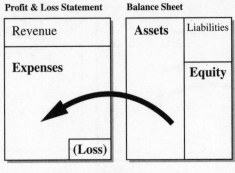

The Bad

Figure 3.9

P&L Statement. If there are substantial assets on the Balance Sheet, the company may use those assets to cover expenses reflected on the P&L. While this is a bad situation long term, the company nevertheless has staying power to ride through the tough times and make necessary adjustments to restore the company to profitability in the future. See Figure 3.9.

When does it get ugly? If the company continues to operate with the bad financial performance just described—that is, a loss on the P&L Statement—the assets reported on the Balance Sheet will eventually be depleted. When that happens, it is a downright dreadful situation. A negative P&L Statement and an insolvent Balance Sheet—a situation where liabilities exceed assets—most often indicate looming disaster. When the company's loss on the P&L Statement has depleted the company's assets such that liabilities outnumber assets on the Balance Sheet, the company must then find money from an outside source. And raising cash by selling assets or borrowing against them is difficult, if not impossible, because there are few assets remaining and no financial strength to attract a lender. Enter government bailout or bankruptcy protection, because failing these measures, the game is over. See Figure 3.10.

Scary? In an economy of slowing sales, tightening credit, and fading consumer confidence, an employee who works toward

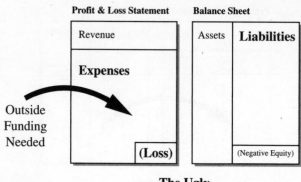

Figure 3.10

reversing such ugly financial situations is indispensable. That employee could be you.

No matter what economy you find yourself in, and because the economy is always changing, I recommend that you continue your financial education. There are countless books on this topic, but one of my favorite references that you should have on your shelf is the book *Financial Intelligence* by Karen Berman and Joe Knight with John Case.

What's Next?

Congratulations! You now have financial knowledge and ability that most people don't have, which means that you have the skills necessary to be indispensable. If you apply what you have learned, you will be worth substantially more to your company (or any prospective company) than you were before reading this book. So the question is: What are you going to do next?

Afterword

What *Else* Is in It for You?

A funny thing happened after I finished writing this book. I found something else you should know about, so I'm adding it in just before my deadline for final manuscript submission. It compliments the concepts and principles I conveyed in *Indispensable by Monday* so well that it seems a natural exclamation point, and I had to include it. I hope you find it useful.

You have learned how to improve the financial status of your employer. Now, what about your family finances? You can apply these same concepts to improve your home Profit and Loss Statement and Balance Sheet. After all, activities like reducing your own expenses and increasing your family's income provide the same advantages for your cash flow and net worth as cost-cutting and revenue enhancing do for your company's bottom line.

Although the concepts are the same, the financial practices and objectives used at your work are often different from the ones you will apply at home. At work, decisions about what to do with money are made by leaders and owners who rely on staff, committees, and outside experts—all in a strictly business context. At home, these decisions are made by you—with a different set of goals. To maximize your financial success at home, you will need to access the best sources of knowledge and expertise in personal financial affairs. Recently, I found just such a source.

Go to www.moneydesktop.com and you will discover the most comprehensive online debt elimination and personal wealth management system that I have seen. My friend Mike introduced me to this company, which has spent four years and several million dollars developing this system. Mike, who knew about Money Desktop and read an early draft of my book, quickly concluded that the same concepts in business that I am teaching can be applied to help individuals with their personal finances at home using the Money Desktop system. Having thoroughly evaluated this product, I agree with Mike and would like to recommend it to you. It is a robust tool that will organize and track your finances, with useful functions to help you quickly reduce debt (as quickly as in one-third the time) and build wealth. One of the features you may like most is a what-if utility that, much like the Profit Proposal Generator you use at work, calculates the financial impact of ideas you may want to implement at home, such as refinancing a mortgage or the result of buying versus leasing a car, as just two examples.

My only reservation in recommending the Money Desktop system is that as of this writing it is not free. However, if you check it out, I think you will agree that the system is impressive, and helpful enough to more than justify the small monthly charge. Having said that, it's my pleasure to tell you that I have asked Money Desktop's management team to allow my readers to use the system FREE OF CHARGE. They graciously agreed. The more users they can serve, the more quickly news of their product's benefits will spread during the early stages of its launch. So, go to www.moneydesktop.com and use the code: WEDNESDAY to get the free and full use of a very powerful system for eliminating debt, building wealth, and improving your own P&L Statement and Balance Sheet. I have been assured that this offer will be honored for at least the first 20,000 subscribers who use this code.

I'd like to know how this product works for you and if you think I should continue to recommend it to others. Please send any feedback to info@moreorlessinc.com.

If you choose to pursue this personal approach to fiscal responsibility, please do so *after* you become indispensable at work, which as you know is scheduled for Monday. Shoot for financial indispensability at home by, say, Wednesday evening at around 8:00 PM.

Best wishes for your financial success at work *and* at home,

Larry Myler

About the Author

For 30 years, Larry Myler has been building businesses. He has founded six companies on his own or with partners and has consulted for clients ranging from start-ups to the Fortune 500. He served as the president of VitalSmarts, an organizational development training firm, for over nine years. As CEO of the profit-enhancement firm More or Less, Inc., Larry continues to create profit and build financial strength for clients worldwide. Larry has a BS in psychology from Brigham Young University and an MBA with an emphasis in international business from the University of Utah.

He and his wife, Jill, are the proud parents of three and (even prouder) grandparents of one. They live in Utah and enjoy the beauty of the Rocky Mountains year-round.

Notes

1. Victor S.L. Tan, "The Dangers of Complacency," March 16, 2004. Available at: http://www.scribd.com/doc/7566453/The-Dangers-of-Complacency.
2. Alan G. Robinson and Sam Stern, *Corporate Creativity: How Innovation and Improvement Actually Happen* (San Francisco, CA: Berrett-Koehler, 1998).
3. Carol Gelderman, *Henry Ford: The Wayward Capitalist* (New York: Dial Press, 1981).
4. Kim Hart, "Angry Customers Use Web to Shame Firms," *Washington Post*, July 5, 2006.
5. Michael S. Wood, "What If We Just Said, 'I'm Sorry'?" *Patient Safety and Quality Healthcare*, November/December 2005. Available at: http://www.psqh.com/novdec05/what-if.html. Also see Insurance Information Institute, "Medical Malpractice," October 2009. Available at: http://www.iii.org/media/hottopics/insurance/medicalmal/#.
6. Dan Malachowski, "Wasted Time at Work Costing Companies Billions," July 2005. Available at: http://www.salary.com/careers/layouthtmls/crel_display_nocat_Ser374_Par555.htm.
7. Liz Webber, "Average Employee Wastes Two Hours of Every Workday," *Inc.*, July 30, 2007. Available at: http://www.inc.com/news/articles/200707/time.html.
8. Websense, "Surfing the Web at Work May Be as Addictive as Cup of Joe," May 9, 2005. Available at: http://www.websense.com/global/en/PressRoom/PressReleases/PressReleaseDetail/?Release=050509928. Also see Tech Crunchies: Internet Statistics and Numbers, "How Long Do People Surf Internet at Work?" December 15, 2007. Available at: http://techcrunchies.com/how-long-do-people-surf-internet-at-work/.

9. Eric Fox, "The Importance of the Cash Conversion Cycle," October 10, 2008. Available at: http://stocks.investopedia.com/stock-analysis/2008/the-importance-of-the-cash-conversion-cycle-hov-kbh-tol1010.aspx.

10. Barry Jaruzelski, Conrad Winkler, and Eric Dustman, "$950 Billion in Extra Capital," *Strategy and Business*, Summer, 2009, Issue 55.

11. WorldatWork, *2008–09, Salary Budget Survey* (Scottsdale, AZ: WorldatWork, 2009).

12. Mean average inflation rate, 1997 through 2008, available at: http://www.inflationdata.com.

13. See Burton A. Weisbrod, Jeffrey P. Ballou, and Evelyn D. Asch, *Mission and Money: Understanding the University* (Cambridge: Cambridge University Press, 2008); p. 77, which acknowledges that the slogan "no margin, no mission" is frequently used by nonprofits.

14. Alex Dichter, Fredrik Lind, and Seelan Singham, "Turning around a Struggling Airline: An Interview with the CEO of Malaysia Airlines," *McKinsey Quarterly*, November 2008.

Index